Computing Texts

A Java notebook

A first course in programming

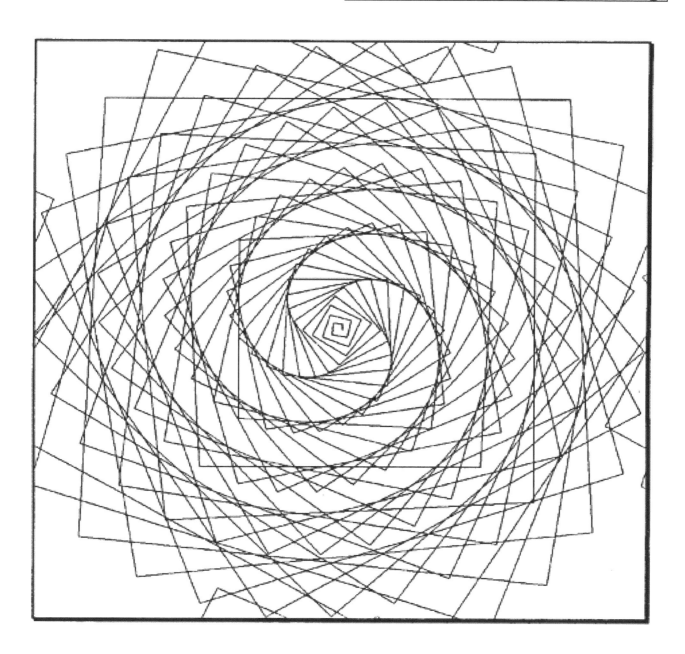

Tony Hawken

ISBN 978-1-4457-4511-4

Preface

Aim

The aim of this book is to introduce programming to students who possibly haven't programmed before. The vehicle chosen for this is the Java programming language. It is based on a number of units validated by OCNLR for an Access to Higher Education diploma in computing.

More specifically there are 2 level-3 units that I have based this book on. They are:

1. Computer programming concepts using Java Course-code: CK3/3/LN/011
2. Programming for the Internet using Java applets. Course-code: CD0/3/LN/110

The first of these is worth 6 credits. That is it is a double unit course. I have split this unit into two parts. They appear in part 1 and part 2 of this book. Also within this, there is a requirement to write applets as well as Java applications. I have left this out of parts 1 and 2 of the book, as applet programming is covered in part 3 of the book. Otherwise parts 1 and 2 of this book cover the assessment requirements for the unit "Computer programming concepts using Java".

The second unit listed – "Programming for the Internet using Java" has a credit-value of 3. This is a single unit, and is covered in part 3 of the book.

Although intended primarily for an Access to Higher Education diploma in computing, I should note that there are other level 3 courses that offer Java programming for a number of optional units. The prime example that comes to mind is the BTEC National certificate and diploma in Information Technology. This book is also suitable for a foundation year at university.

This book intends to provide a sound foundation for those students intending to study Computer Science or related courses at university. Java is the language of choice for most universities teaching Computer Science. In a number of universities to my knowledge, the material in this book easily covers what is taught in the first year.

Origins

Quite a number of years ago, I started teaching computing on an Access to Higher Education course. The language used at the time was Pascal. Even then I considered this choice of language outdated and inappropriate. I wanted a language that students would continue to use at university, or would at least provide transferable skills. Then as now, both C++ and Java tended to be the language of choice for a first course in programming. At the time I chose C++ as it was easy to modify the units on Pascal to C++ without much effort.

Since leaving teaching it had come to my attention that it is difficult to find teachers to teach Java on an Access to Higher education program. This book is intended as support for teachers who have to teach such units.

I first taught a number of courses in Java in 2000. Since then the language has advanced considerably, so that many of the programs I wrote then, would possibly not work or at least would seem dated. In particular when writing GUI applications I used the AWT package. Now it is expected that where possible you will use swing components. Every year the language is updated. New features are added to the language and certain older features are retired or deprecated. It is for this reason that I felt it was time to reacquaint myself with Java to get up-to-date. Writing this book has provided the motivation.

Approach

The material in this book is designed to be informal and easy to use. It is a very practical "How to do" book, where the emphasis is trying things out. There is very little theory – just enough, in my opinion to make sense. The bulk of the book is made up of example programs with brief notes to explain how the programs work. There are in some cases introductory notes that appear before the example programs, and there are exercises to work from in addition.

There are 3 parts to this book. Each part corresponds to a module taught on the Access to computing diploma. These parts are divided up into 5 chapters or weeks. Each chapter should take a week to complete. This involves 3 hours of teaching per week in college, and between 2 and 3 hours homework per week. The 3 hours teaching per week at college should involve about 40% practical work. That is, writing programs, the remainder being used for lecture.

There is possibly too much material in the book. This is intentional, as it provides more scope for the more able student. Any teacher who adopts this book for use in a class should be aware of this. It is possible that they will choose to omit sections. The extra material will allow for differentiated teaching.

Resources

The book uses the Java Development Kit. This can be downloaded free from the Internet. I would recommend that colleges download and install this software even if they intend using some other programming environment. It is possible to download a Java IDE to do all the programming.

Besides the Java JDK, I have made use of Microsoft Word and OpenOffice for producing the text of this book. The images have been cropped and saved using Microsoft Paint, and any mathematical expressions have been typed in using WinTeXmacs.

This book makes no pretences at being complete, and in many cases may be too brief. For that reason, it is recommended that other books are consulted – see the bibliography for suggestions.

Contents

Part 3   Programming for the Internet using applets

Part 1

Computer programming with Java

Aims

After completing this 5-week unit, you will be able to do the following:

Data

Describe the different data types available in Java, explaining how they can be used.

Declare and use variables. Use of variables includes assignment and applying arithmetic operators to them.

Input and output

Write simple working programs that include suitable input and output that is suitably formatted.

Control structures

Identify and use appropriate selection methods to solve particular programming problems.

Identify and use appropriate iteration methods. These should include both definite and indefinite loops.

Style and documentation

Write clear programs that are well laid out with consistent indentation.

Document your program by including appropriate comments.

Errors and testing

Have knowledge about the different types of error that are likely to occur, and be able to interpret error messages and correct the errors.

Be able to describe the importance of testing and know of some techniques for testing your programs. Apply at least one of these to test your programs.

week1

An introduction to Java programming

1.1 Introduction

The aim of this course is to give a practical introduction to the Java programming language. Each week you will be expected to attend and write programs.

This week we will be looking at the prerequisites to programming in Java and making a start to the course.

You will be expected to:

1. Gain an appreciation of why Java is currently the most sought after IT skill.

2. Know how to use an editor and be able to enter simple DOS commands at a DOS prompt

3. Understand the Java development environment.

4. Edit, compile and execute a simple Java application.

5. Edit, compile and execute a simple Java applet.

6. Write simple Java applications that demonstrate simple output

7. Write programs that can allocate storage and perform calculations

1.2 Why Java?

Java is a platform independent, object-oriented programming language. It was developed by James Gosling at Sun Microsystems and released in 1995. It has been primarily used on the World Wide Web. It is however a general-purpose language that has much in common with C++.

It is currently the main language taught in universities to Computer Science students and has now overtaken C++ as the most popular language in the computer industry. For many years, languages such as C and C++ have appealed to universities because of their portability. Introductory courses could be offered on most types of computer hardware provided a suitable compiler for the language existed. Portability could be achieved, provided that accepted standards within the language were maintained. This has always been the case with both C, and C++.

Neglecting any considerations of design the development process involves:

1. Coding - typing in the program (Source code) using a suitable editor.
2. Compiling - translating the source code into machine code (for a particular machine/operating system)
3. Linking - Loading appropriate libraries and routines etc to make the machine code executable.
4. Testing and debugging

In the above example (i.e. that of C and C++ it is only the source code which is truly portable. If a particular application written in either C or C++ were to be run on a different computer platform, the source code would have to be recompiled using a compiler for the particular machine and operating system.

Java continues in the same tradition as C and C++, but offers new dimensions to the idea of portability. The Java programming language achieves portability by means of The Java Virtual Machine (JVM).

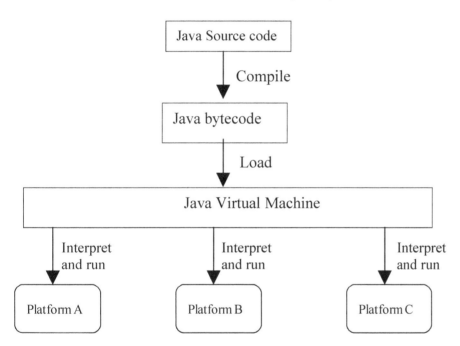

In the above, compilation of Java source code produces an intermediate code (called bytecode) that can be interpreted by any computer that has the JVM installed. That is, you can run Java bytecode on any computer that has Java installed on it.

The product we will be using is the JDK (Java Development Kit). This is recognised as the de-facto standard for Java programming and furthermore is free. It can be obtained either by buying a Java book that includes a CD-ROM, or by downloading from the Internet. Most universities use this product, as do many businesses. This, and the fact that growth in the Internet started to take place shortly after Java first began to be used, explains the phenomenal growth in the popularity of Java.

Java is an object-oriented language, unlike C++ which is a hybrid language. This means that you will have to use classes and objects when you write Java programs. If you write programs using C++ you can choose to write procedural style, or object-oriented style programs - or perhaps a bit of both.

It is often said that Java is simpler than C++. In my opinion this just isn't true. It is true that pointers, memory management and overloaded operators have been omitted. Memory management in Java is done automatically, which is a very useful feature, and it is true that pointers are difficult to use properly in C++. Not having overloaded operators however removes a very nice feature of C++, which helps explain why all input in Java is horrendously complicated - especially when compared with C++.

It is also said that Java is a small language in the same manner that C or C++ are small languages. All of these languages can only be considered to be small languages if you only use a core of the language which excludes using any program libraries. In the case of Java, especially when you include all the class libraries, it is an incredibly large language. This you will conclude when you see the size of most Java books.

Probably the main reason why Java is so popular is the relation of Java to the web. It is relatively easy to write programs for the Internet, and that can access databases. It is particularly popular for web-servers because it is one of the few programming languages that offer any form of security. Writing programs that use a graphical user interface is also relatively easy using Java.

Java can be considered a secure language, firstly because it is difficult to execute code that produces damaging results. One reason for this is the exclusion of pointers. Also, Java programs are compiled into bytecode. Before this bytecode can be run, it is verified by the interpreter to check that there is nothing suspicious in the program. There are also severe restrictions as to what can be done by applets on other peoples systems.

1.3 Practical Skills required

Rather than include a detailed discussion of necessary prerequisites I have included a checklist of useful skills. Some of these are also illustrated below.

1. Open and close folders

2. Resize and move windows

3. Be able to create objects such as folders and shortcuts

4. Know how to use an editor such as notepad

5. Know how to obtain a DOS prompt

6. Be able to Enter DOS commands

7. Know how to use a word-processor such as Microsoft Word

8. Be able to use a search engine to find information on the internet

Some of these required skills will be illustrated in this section.

Creating new folders or short cuts

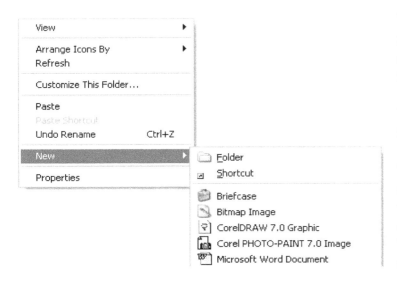

You can obtain the drop-down menu on the right by clicking on the right button of your mouse.

We will be choosing to create new folders or new shortcuts

You will need a new folder for each unit in this book. Within these folders you may need separate folders for programs, Word documents, and items downloaded from the Internet.

New folder

If you click on the folder option, you get a new folder like this. You can choose a name for your folder by typing in a name at this stage. Later on you can rename the folder by right-clicking on the folder icon – then choose the rename option. In a similar manner you can delete folders etc.

New shortcut

In this example I will demonstrate how to create a shortcut for notepad. First of all you have to find where it is located. If you use Windows XP, you click on the following: Start → All programs → Accessories → Notepad → Properties.

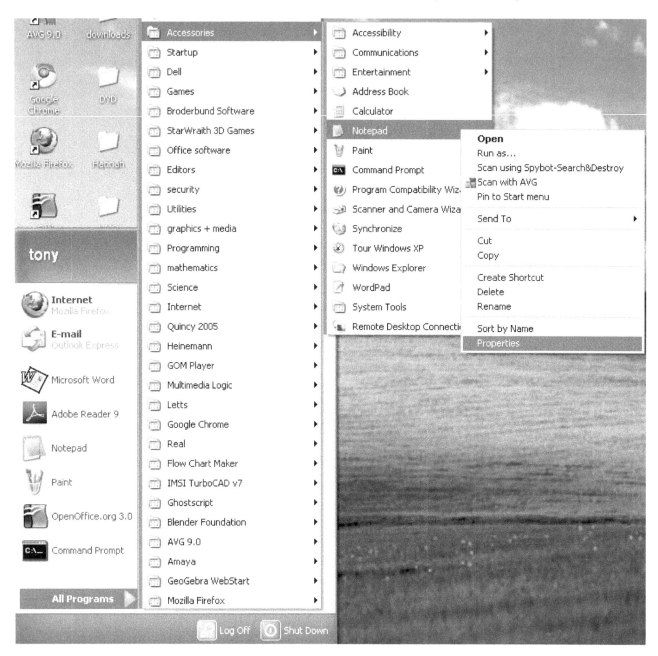

Clicking on properties gives you Window on the left (1). What we're interested in, is the target address for notepad. If you right-click your mouse you can save this address.

This value can be used later when we create the shortcut. Right-click your mouse in the current folder, and select the shortcut option to get (2). Then click within the text box where you have to enter the location of the file. Now right-click your mouse and click on Paste. The previously saved target address is now used to create the shortcut.

(1) Notepad properties

(2) Creating a shortcut

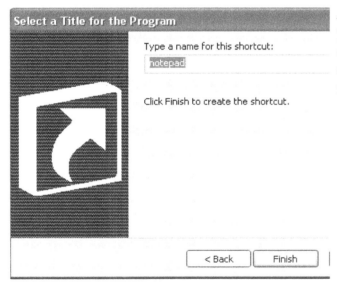

Assuming the correct address has been pasted in, the software will be identified as Notepad. All you have to do now is click on Finish. You then obtain the following shortcut.

You should also create a shortcut to the command prompt (cmd). You will also locate this in accessories. So, now you have a shortcut to notepad. You will use this to create Java programs. The command prompt is required to compile and run your Java programs.

Enter DOS commands

If you are writing programs for a PC with a Windows operating system you need to be able to obtain a command prompt. This enables you to enter MS-DOS commands, just like on the old computers before Windows.

When you execute cmd (the command prompt program) you obtain something like this.

You are advised to create a shortcut for this program in your current working folder where you are going to write Java programs.

I will be indicating some of the commands that you will possibly need.

Change drive. Your hard disk is probably partitioned (2 – 4 drives). Each partition then will be referred to as C:(C drive), D:, E:, and F: etc. If you want to change to the E drive, you enter **E:**. You will then get the prompt **E:>**.

Change folder (folders used to be called directories). This is done using the CD command. Entering **CD javadev** will move you to a folder called **javadev** in the current folder. Entering **CD /javadev** will move you to a folder called **javadev** in the root directory.

Listing files. A listing of all files in the current folder can be obtained by entering **DIR**.

You can use wild cards to match specific types of file. The command **DIR *.java** will match all the files that contain Java source code.

Clear the screen. Enter **CLS** to clear the screen.

In particular we will want to be able to use the command prompt to be able to compile and run our Java programs. This will be explained later.

Exercise 1-1

1. Explain the terms Compiler, Interpreter, Source code, and bytecode.

2. List five DOS commands that you feel would be useful for this course. Describe what they do. The actions of some of these commands can be reproduced in Windows mode. Where possible describe how.

3. Locate the official Java web site. Locate one or more pages that document the Java language.

4. Use the Internet to find a source of Java programming tutorials. Write down the URLs of all those sites that contain useful sources of material.

5. Create a folder called **javadev**. Within this folder create a shortcut for **notepad** and another for **cmd**.

1.4 The Java development environment

As I have already stated, the JDK can either be obtained by buying a book with the appropriate CD-ROM containing the JDK, or alternatively it can be obtained via the Internet. To download this product from the official Java web site enter the address:

http:/www.javasoft.com

This brings up the Java home page. On it you will find a list of products which can be downloaded. There are many different products intended for different computer platforms.

The file that you obtain as a result from a download, or from a CD-ROM is a self-extracting compressed file. To perform an installation all you have to do is double click the icon corresponding to this file.

The Java Development Kit (JDK) consists of a collection of programs and documentation that enable developers to compile, run and debug Java programs.

The main programs are listed below:

1. The compiler (`javac`) - translates the source code into Java bytecode

2. The interpreter (`java`) - reads the bytecode of a compiled Java application and runs it.

3. The applet viewer (`appletviewer`) - used to run compiled Java applets.

4. The decompiler (`javap`) - reads Java byte code and produces an outline description of the source code.

5. A debugger (`jdb`) - helps detect bugs in Java programs.

6. Java documentation generator (`javadoc`) - reads declarations and comments, and produces HTML pages describing the classes used in a program.

1.5 Edit, Compile and Execute a simple Java application

A Java program can be one of two kinds.

1. An application is a general-purpose program that can be interpreted using the Java interpreter.

2. An applet is a Java program that has to be run from a browser.

Most of the programs that we will be writing will be applications.

To create a Java program you need to use an editor. We will be using the Windows editor called notepad. You could use a word-processor such as Microsoft Word, but if you do you must be extremely careful to save the file as a text file. Make sure that the file is saved with a `.java` extension, not `.java.txt`.

The following is an example of a simple Java program:

<u>Example 1</u>

```
public class example1
{
    public static void main(String [] args)
    {
        System.out.println("My first Java program !");
    }
}
```

When typing Java programs you should note that all Java programs are case-sensitive, and should a keyword be miss-spelt or be in the wrong case the program will not compile. You should note from the above that most characters are in lower-case, and you should find that this is true for most Java programs.

The above program should be saved with the name

```
example1.java
```

The name of the saved program should always be the same as that of the class with a .java extension.

To compile a program you need to use a DOS prompt such as that below:

```
E:\JavaDev>
```

In this case I have changed to the E: drive. This can be achieved by entering **E:**

I have also changed to a different directory of folder by entering the DOS command **CD javadev.**

Now enter the command: `javac example1.java`

to compile the Java source code.

Using the cmd prompt

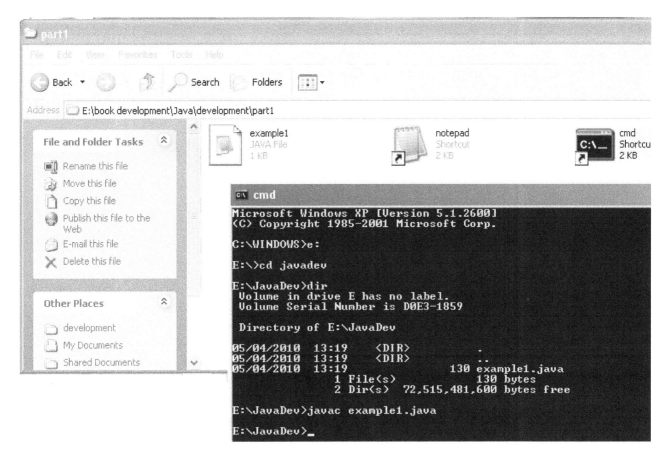

From this source code, byte code will be produced. This will be stored in a file called **example1.class**.

You can execute the byte code stored in example1.class by entering the command:

```
java example1.class
```

    or just

```
java example1
```

running the program

1.6 Edit, compile and execute a simple Java applet

The source code for a Java applet is created in the same way as an application. That is you use an editor such as notepad and type it in. Remember to save it as a text file and with the extension **.java**.

An example of a Java applet follows:

Example 2

```
import javax.swing.JApplet;
import java.awt.Graphics;

public class app1 extends JApplet
{
    public void paint(Graphics g)
    {
        g.drawString("A first applet !", 5, 25);
    }
}
```

For this particular program, it must be saved with the name **app1.java**.

The applet source code is compiled in the same way as for an application. For the above code we would type in the command

```
javac app1.java
```

Java applets need to be run from an HTML document. An example follows:

Example 3

```
<HTML>
<HEAD>
<TITLE>My first applet</TITLE>
</HEAD>
<BODY>
This is the output from my first applet
<BR>
<APPLET CODE="app1.class" WIDTH=200 HEIGHT=50>
</APPLET>
</BODY>
</HTML>
```

HTML documents such as the one above are also typed in using an ordinary editor such as notepad. They are text files which are saved with the extension **.html**.

We are now in a position to view the output using appletviewer (or some other Java-enabled browser). To use appletviewer to run the applet, type in the following:

```
appletviewer app1.html
```

The output should look like this:

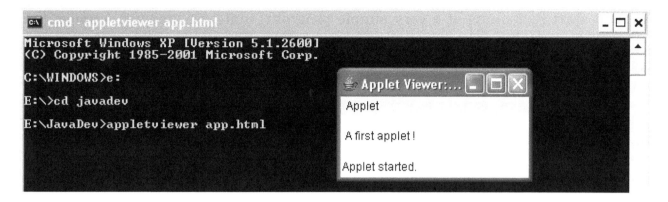

If you double click on the icon for the html file you obtain the following output.

Exercise 1-2

1. Distinguish between a Java application and an applet.

2. What do the following acronyms stand for - IDE, GUI, JDK, JIT, JVM, API, HTML

3. Distinguish between a **.java** and a **.class** file.

4. Type in, compile and run the previous Java Application (Example 1).

5. Type in and compile the Java applet illustrated previously (Example 2).

6. Run the applet (Example 2) using appletviewer.

7. Type in the example HTML code (Example 3). Load this to run the applet.

1.7   A first attempt at programming

We will start by looking at a very simple program, that just displays a single line of text.

Example 4

```java
//    Program saved as prog1.java

public class prog1
{
    public static void main( String  args[] )
    {
        System.out.println("This is my first Java program ");
    }
}
```

```
cmd

E:\JavaDev>java prog1
This is my first Java program

E:\JavaDev>_
```

Notes:

1. The first line is a single line or C++ style comment. The comment does nothing except provide documentation and make the program more readable.

2. **public class prog1** is used to begin a class definition. Every program must have at least one of these.

3. The name of the file that you save the program must be based on the class name. In this case it should be called prog1.java.

4. Every Java application has at least one method or function. Exactly one of these must be called **main()**.

5. The main function header always has the format

    ```java
    public static void main(String [] args)
    ```

6. The keyword **public** denotes the fact that the method **main()** can be accessed by all other classes.

7. The keyword **static** is used to say that the method being defined applies to the class itself rather than the objects of the class.

8. The keyword **void** is used to tell us that the method **main()** has no return values.

9. Curly brackets { } are used to contain a block of code.

10. The line

    ```
    System.out.println("This is my first Java program ");
    ```

    prints out a single line of text. In this case the text is the contents of a literal string – that is everything between the double quotes. The cursor then moves to the next line ready for the next line of text to be printed.

11. There is a print method in Java that is similar to `println` except that the cursor does not move onto the next line. A `print` or `println` statement that follows will continue on the same line in the current position.

12. The semi-colon ';' is a statement terminator. Every statement within a Java program must have one.

13. The following is another example of a comment (C style comment):

    ```
    /*   This comment can fit over many lines.
         The comment will continue until the closing
         delimiter is found                              */
    ```

14. White space and blank lines are also ignored by the compiler. Addition of blank lines and white space often makes the program more readable.

15. Often your program won't compile because you have an error of syntax. These are often called compile-time errors because they occur when you are compiling the program. The illustration below indicates what you will see if you miss out the semi-colon from the previous program.

16. At other times, your program will compile, but will fail to run properly. It either does not run at all or produces the wrong output. This is called a run-time error as it occurs when you are running the program. Getting the wrong output, is also called a logic error.

1.8   Allocating storage in Java

1.8.1   Primitive data types in Java

There are 8 primitive data types in Java.

boolean	either true or false
char	a 2 byte Unicode character
byte	1 byte of storage for storing very small integers
short	a 2 byte integer
int	a 4 byte integer
long	an 8 byte integer
float	a 4 byte real number
double	an 8 byte real number

A **boolean** is used to store one of two values – true or false.

A **char** is considered to be a very small number, as it takes up only 2 bytes of storage. Each character is represented by a number – represented using Unicode. In languages such as C or C++ a char is only one byte and is represented using **ASCII**.

The ASCII character set only codes 256 different characters. The ASCII character set is in fact a subset of the Unicode character set. As Unicode has two bytes of storage, many more characters can be stored. This includes Chinese, Japanese and Korean characters.

An integer is a whole number. They can be negative or positive. The keywords **byte** and **int** are used to declare storage for storing integers. A **byte** is extremely small and is only used to store very small numbers. Mostly, people use the **int** data type when they want to store an integer.

The keywords **short** and **long** are data type modifiers used with the **int** keyword. An **int** usually takes up four bytes of storage, whereas **long int**, typically takes up 8 bytes of storage.

Both **floats** and **double** are used to store floating point numbers. These are used to represent real numbers. In computing terms a real number is merely a number that needs a decimal point in it. This would be called a rational number in mathematics. The double type has a greater precision than that of a float. That is you can represent a number with many more numbers after the decimal point.

1.8.2   Variable declaration

A **variable** is a named location in memory and is used to store a value. The amount of storage allocated to a variable depends on the variable type. So for instance the statement

```
int num;
```

will allocate 4 bytes of storage to the memory location referred to as num. Also, this variable is to be used to store an integer value (number of type int). So, you cannot for instance store a data value of type float here, even though an int and a float require the same amount of memory for storage.

You can also store a value in a variable when you declare it. When you do this, it is said that the variable has been initialized. In the following example:

```
float amount = 13.75;
```

4 bytes of storage is allocated and given a name amount. This storage is only suitable for storing data of type float. The value 13.75 is then stored in this variable. `

The following are valid statements used to declare variables:

```
int x, y, z, sum;    //Create 4 integers
char ans = 'y' ;     //Create a char and store the letter a
float average;       //Create a float called average
boolean success;     //create a boolean called success
```

1.8.3   Naming variables

When you declare variables the following rules must be obeyed

- All variables need to be declared before they are used.

- A variable name cannot be a Java keyword (reserved word)

- Variable names must begin with a letter, an underscore character (_), or a dollar sign ($). For the programs in this book, all variables will start with a letter.

- Subsequent letters in a variable name may only include letters, numeric digits, underscore or a dollar sign.

- There can be no spaces within a variable name.

The following rules are a matter of programming style. They are not mandatory, just good practice.

- Where possible, a variable should be entirely in lowercase.

- Where a variable name is made up of two words joined together, the start of the second word should be in uppercase. E.g. nettPay is a suitable variable for storing the your pay minus tax paid.

1.8.4   Variable assignment

Assignment is used to store data in a variable. The **assignment** operator is denoted by **=**.

The following are valid assignment statements.

```
x = 3; y = 2; z = 5;
ans = 'y';
ans = 64;
average = (x + y + z)/ 3.0;
success = true;
int a = 5;
double pi = 3.14159;
```

Notes:

1.   `x = 3;`   stores the value 3 in the variable called x.

2.   `ans = 'y';`   stores the character constant y. Note single quotes are required for character constants.

3.   `ans = 64;`   Stores the character with ASCII code 64.

4.   `average = (x + y + z) / 3.0;`   Computes RHS and stores the result in average. Need to use 3.0 rather than 3 for floating-point division.

5.   `success = true;`   Stores the boolean value true in the variable success.

There now follows an example program that illustrates the declaration, assignment and display of primitive data types within Java.

Example 5

```
// A demonstration of primitive data types in Java

public class datatypes
{    public static void main(String [] args)
     {
          // declare and initialise variables
          boolean b = true;
          char c = 'A';           // 'A' is a character constant
          byte d = 100;
          short e = 3500;
          int f = 365000;
          long g = 12345678912345L;     // 'L' is for long
          float h = 3.14159F;           // 'F' is for float
```

18

```
        double pi = 3.141592653589793;

        // Output content of variables
        System.out.println("b = " + b);
        System.out.println("c = " + c);
        System.out.println("d = " + d);
        System.out.println("e = " + e);
        System.out.println("f = " + f);
        System.out.println("g = " + g);
        System.out.println("h = " + h);
        System.out.println("pi = " + pi);
    }
}
```

```
cmd

E:\JavaDev>javac datatypes.java

E:\JavaDev>java datatypes
b = true
c = A
d = 100
e = 3500
f = 365000
g = 12345678912345
h = 3.14159
pi = 3.141592653589793

E:\JavaDev>_
```

Notes:

1. Variables need to be declared before they are used.

2. Variables can be initialized when they are declared. That is, they are given a value when they are declared

3. Variables can be assigned a value at a later date if required.

4. A variable must begin with an alphabetic character and is usually lower-case.

5. A Java variable cannot be a reserved word. The following are reserved words in Java:

   abstract, assert, boolean, break, byte, case, catch, char, class, const, continue, default, do, double, else, extends, false, final, finally, float, for, goto, if, implements, import, instanceof, int, interface, long, native, new, null, package, private, protected, public, return, short, static, strictfp, super, switch, synchronised, this, throw, throws, transient, true, try, void, volatile, while

6. The concatenate operator '+' is used to append the value of a variable to the end of a literal string.

1.9   Simple arithmetic

When solving simple problems in arithmetic using pen and paper we often write down an expression which summarises how the numbers are to be combined.

e.g. $\dfrac{9 \times 25}{5} + 32$

We can make this expression more general by using letters in place of one or more of the numbers. These letters being used are called variables and are there in our expression to represent any number we may wish to substitute.

So for instance we could have a more general expression

$\dfrac{9 \times c}{5} + 32$

and we could indicate that we wish to make a substitution by writing let c = 5. We can do the same thing in Java, but would instead write such expressions as:

9 * 25 / 5 + 32

or

c = 25;
9 * c / 5 + 32

We often want to write this as an equation giving a name to the result that we have just worked out.

i.e. $f = \dfrac{9 \times c}{5} + 32$

This is exactly what we do in our program.

```
c = 25;                  // store 25 in c (substitution)

f = 9 * c / 5  + 32;     // Multiply c by 9, divide by 5 and
                         // add 32. Then store the result in f
```

The previous two statements are called assignment statements because values are being assigned or given to variables. The '=' character is referred to as the assignment operator.

We are now in a position to complete a program that demonstrates simple use of arithmetic.

Example 6

```
// Convert Centigrade to Fahrenheit

public class temp
{
    public static void main(String [] args)
    {
        float c, f;
        c = 25;
        f = 9/5 * c + 32;
        System.out.print("C = " + c);
        System.out.println("\t F = " + f);
    }
}
```

```
cmd

E:\JavaDev>java temp
C = 25.0            F = 57.0

E:\JavaDev>
```

Notes:

1. **System** is a class in the package **java.lang**

2. **System.out** is a symbolic constant that refers to the screen

3. **System.out.print** is a method that displays text on the screen without moving the cursor to a new line

4. **System.out.println** is a method that displays text on a screen, but moves the cursor to a new line afterwards

5. The escape sequence **\t** is used to print a tab

Below is a table summarising the arithmetic operators available in Java.

Operator	Name	Example	Result
+	add	3 + 8	11
-	subtract	27 -3	24
*	multiply	7 * 4	28
/	divide	35 / 7	5
%	modulus	24 / 5	4

When the calculations get more complicated we need to worry about the order of evaluating arithmetic expressions. If we concern ourselves with only the above arithmetic operators, the order of evaluating an expression (precedence of operations) is the same as you learnt in mathematics.

For your convenience, the precedence of the arithmetic operators that we are considering are summarised below:

Operator

Precedence

```
()                      brackets
*    /    %             multiply, divide, modulus
+    -                  add, subtract
```

Example 7

```java
// A demonstration of arithmetic operators in Java

public class arith
{    public static void main(String [] args)
     {
             int a = 11, b = 4;
             int sum = a + b;
             System.out.println("Sum = " + sum);
             int difference = a - b;
             System.out.println("Difference = " + difference);
             int product = a * b;
             System.out.println("Product = " + product);
             int quotient = a / b;
             System.out.println("Quotient = " + quotient);
             int remainder = a % b;
             System.out.println("remainder = " + remainder);
     }
}
```

```
c:\  cmd

E:\JavaDev>java arith
Sum = 15
Difference = 7
Product = 44
Quotient = 2
remainder = 3

E:\JavaDev>_
```

Notes:

1. When integers are combined using the arithmetic operators, the result is always an integer.

2. In ordinary division, when you divide two numbers there is often an answer that is not an integer. In a Java program, if the operands are integers, the remainder is truncated leaving an integer result.

3. The remainder operator obtains the remainder when one number is divided by another.

There follows a practical example that uses both integer division and the remainder function. In this example we are converting a value in cm to km, m, and cm.

Example 8

```
// A demonstration of integer division and integer remainder

public class integerdiv
{      public static void main(String [] args)
       {
              int cm = 275650;

              int km = cm / 100000;     // integer division - extract km
              cm = cm % 100000;     //save remainder after extracting km
              int m = cm / 100;     //integer division - extract m
              cm = cm % 100;     //save remainder - leaves cm left over

              // Output resuts
              System.out.println("Number of km : " + km);
              System.out.println("Number of m  : " + m);
              System.out.println("Number of cm : " + cm);
       }
}
```

```
C:\ cmd

E:\JavaDev>java integerdiv
Number of km : 2
Number of m  : 756
Number of cm : 50

E:\JavaDev>
```

Notes:

1.   The result of the division given by **km = cm / 100000;** will be an integer, because both cm and 100000 are integers.

2.   The statement **cm = cm % 100000;** will divide the current value of cm by 100000 and store the remainder in cm.

3.   The integer division **cm / 100** will extract the number of metres.

4.   The expression **c % 100** will extract the remainder. That is the number of cm left over once the number of metres has been subtracted.

1.10   Escape sequences

There are other escape sequences that can be used within a **print** or **println** statement.

Escape character	Output
\n	newline
\t	tab
\b	backspace
\r	carriage return
\f	formfeed
\\	backslash
\'	single quote
\"	double quote
\ddd	octal number
\xdd	hexadecimal number
\udddd	unicode character

Example 9

```
public class esc
{
    public static void main(String [] args)
    {
        System.out.println("This is a\ndemo sentence\non several" +
                        "lines");

        System.out.println("This demonstates the use of tabs" +
                        "\tTony\tHawken\t1\t2");

        System.out.println("This is a quote \"Quote goes here\".");
    }
}
```

```
E:\JavaDev>java esc
This is a
demo sentence
on several lines
This demonstates the use of tabs        Tony    Hawken  1       2
This is a quote "Quote goes here".

E:\JavaDev>
```

Note:

The escape sequences above are just inserted inside the literal string to be displayed using a println statement.

1.11   Assignment, increment and decrement operators

There are a number of assignment operators besides the most used =. For instance, if you want to add 10 to the current value of a variable you could use either of the following statements.

```
x = x + 10;
```

is equivalent to

```
x += 10;
```

The following is a list of the other assignment operators.

```
+=    -=    *=    /=    %=
```

More will be said about these later, when we have a use for them. You can probably guess what they do.

In addition both C, C++, and Java have increment and decrement operators. These work on a single integer value.

Operator	**description**	**example**
++	increment	++a or a++
--	decrement	--a or a--

The statement   `x++;`

is merely a shorthand for the statement   `x = x + 1;`
or   `x += 1;`

That is, add one to the current value of x, then store this new value in x.

You will notice that there are two forms of increment, and two forms of decrement operator. If you compare the two statements below there will be different values stored in y depending on which statement has been executed.

```
//demonstation of pre-increment
int x = 3;
int y = ++x;
```

x	y
3	4

```
//demonstration of post-increment
int x = 3;
int y = x++;
```

x	y
3	3

The pre-decrement and post-decrement operators show the same type of behaviour.

Exercise 1-3

1. Write a program that outputs your name and address on the screen. You can use string literals to do this.

2. Write appropriate declarations to store the following literal values. Where possible choose appropriate variable names.

   a. The character 'A'
   b. The numeric value 1250
   c. The value 12.75
   d. The value 2.456235
   e. The constant π = 3.14159
   f. The Avogadro constant has the value 6.0221367×10^{23}
   g. The name "Tony Hawken"
   h. The 3 exam marks 45, 56 and 62

3. Write a program which will calculate and display the volume of a sphere with a given radius of 7.5cm. Use the formula V = $\frac{4\pi r^3}{3}$ where π = 3.14159.

4. Write Java expressions for the formulae below.

   ## Formulae found in Physics

   ### Laws of motion

   $$(i)\ v = u + at \qquad (ii)\ s = \frac{(u+v)}{2}t \qquad (iii)\ s = ut + \frac{1}{2}at^2$$

   Ohms law

   $$R = \frac{R_1 R_2}{R_1 + R_2}$$

   Coulombs law

   $$F = \frac{kQ_1 Q_2}{r^2}$$

5. Determine the output from the following program.

   ```
   public class demo
   {
       public static void main(String [] args)
       {
           int x = 12;
           int y = 6;
           int p, q;
           p = x % y;
           q = x / y;
           System.out.println("p = " + p);
           System.out.println("q = " + q);
       }
   }
   ```

6. Write a program, so that given a number of days - 235 for instance, you can calculate the exact number of weeks and days left over. Output the result in a suitable format.

7. Fill in the following table to show the current state of each variable as each line of code executes. This type of table is often referred to as a trace table, and may be used for debugging purposes.

Code	x	y	z
int x = 0;			
double y, z = 3.0;			
y = 0.6 * z;			
x = 0.4 * z;			
x = 12;			
y = 3;			
z = x / y;			
x++;			
y = ++x;			
z *= 2;			

8. Examine the following code, and determine the output it would produce.

```java
public class demo2
{
    public static main(String [] args)
    {
        int a = 10;
        int b = 5;
        a *= 5;
        a /= 10;

        System.out.println("a = " + a);
        System.out.println("b = " + b);
    }
}
```

Week 2

Classes, strings and keyboard input

2.1 Classes and objects (a brief introduction)

There are 8 primitive data-types in Java. We can use these data types as in procedural languages to create variables (allocate storage). Every other data-type is derived from a **class** and is called an **object**.

A **class** can be thought of as a template for creating **objects**. Those with experience of either C or C++ programming will know about structures. A **structure** is a purpose built template for a collection of data. In C++ a structure can also be used to define functions which are there to manipulate this collection of data. C++ also has classes which in addition to having data and functions, also define which objects can have access to the data etc.

A Java class is much the same as a class in C++. The data items are usually referred to as **attributes**, and the functions are usually called **methods**. The main difference is that in Java, the program itself is a class. This class can have its own attributes and one or more methods. Exactly one of these methods must be called **main**. It is this method which starts executing first.

You can include additional classes within your program. These additional classes cannot be declared public, and do not contain a method called main, as there can only ever be one method called main in a program.

Each class has one or more special methods that have the same name as the class. These are called **constructors**. One of these constructors will be used each time an object of this type is created.

An **object** is created from a **class** in much the same way as a variable is created from a primitive data-type. When objects are created they can also be assigned values. There are often several ways in which this can be done.

The Java language has many **class libraries** or **packages**. Each class library contains a collection of related classes, which can be used by a programmer to create objects of that type. The collection of class libraries within Java is also referred to as the Java API (Applications Programming Interfaces)

Each class often has many methods to ensure that every conceivable action that is required to process objects of the class type is covered. This means that a Java programmer spends more time using methods that have already been created rather than create their own.

The main packages we will be looking at in this book are:

java.lang	represents the core of the Java language. You don't need to use an import statement to use this.
java.awt	provides windows and graphics facilities to create a graphics-user-interface (gui)
javax.swing	used to create graphics user interfaces with facilities that extend the awt package. This also includes the class JApplet with which we will be creating applets.
java.util	contains general utilities. The one we will commonly be using is the class Scanner.

To be able to access a given package within your program you will need to include one or more import statements.

The statement

```
import java.util.*;
```

will allow you to access all the classes within the `java.util` package.

Whereas the statement

```
import java.util.Scanner
```

Will only allow access to the Scanner class within the package java.util.

2.2   The String class

An object of type String is the simplest type of string available within Java. String objects are immutable. That is once they have data assigned to them they cannot be changed.

There now follows a very short program to illustrate the use of String objects. It demonstrates the use of a number of methods available within the String class.

Example 10

```
public class string1
{public static void main(String[] args)
    {
      String name = "Anthony J. Hawken";
      System.out.println("My name is " + name);
      System.out.println("My name contains " + name.length()+
                  " characters");
      System.out.println("The character at position 4 is " +
                        name.charAt(4));
      System.out.println("The hashcode for my name is " +
                        name.hashCode());
    }
}
```

```
c:\ cmd

E:\JavaDev>java string1
My name is Anthony J. Hawken
My name contains 17 characters
The character at position 4 is o
The hashcode for my name is 657546635

E:\JavaDev>
```

Notes:

1. A string object is implemented as a non-terminated array of characters. You declare a String object in much the same way that you a variable with one of the primitive datatypes.

2. Because String is a class, there are also constructors that you can use to declare String objects.

3. The line:
        String name = "Anthony J. Hawken";

   creates an object called name and allocates "Anthony J. Hawken" to an array within this object. We can also say that the String object name has been initialized.

4. String concatenation we have already seen. This is performed with the '+' operator.

5. `name.length()` - the object **name** calls the method `length()` to compute the length of the string.

6. Like arrays, the index for the first character is zero.

7. `name.charAt(4)` - the object **name** calls the method `charAt()` to determine the character at position 4 in the string. Remember this is the fifth character as the first character has an index value of zero.

8. `name.hashcode()` – the object **name** calls the method `hashcode()` to compute the hash-code of the string.

2.3   Sub-strings

A sub-string is a portion of a given string. You can use the `substring()` method to extract part of a string.

<u>Example 11</u>

```
public class string2
{
  public static void main(String[] args)
  {
      String name = "John Hawken";
      System.out.println(name);
      System.out.println("substring 4 to 8 is " +
                            name.substring(4,8));
      System.out.println("substring 8 to end is " +
                            name.substring(8));
  }
}
```

Notes:

1. The method call `substring(4,8)` extracts the sub-string that starts at character position 4 up to 8. That is is it extracts the 5th, 6th, 7th and 8th characters.

2. The method call `substring(8)` extracts all the characters to the end of the string, starting at the ninth character.

2.4 Other String methods

2.4.1 Changing case

```
toLowerCase()          Converts calling string object to Lower case
toUpperCase()          Converts calling string object to Upper case
```

Example 12

```
public class UpperCaseDemo
{
    public static void main(String [] args)
    {
        String name = "Tony Hawken";

        System.out.println("Name in upper case is " +
                            name.toUpperCase());
    }
}
```

```
C:\ cmd

E:\JavaDev>java UpperCaseDemo
Name in upper case is TONY HAWKEN

E:\JavaDev>_
```

Notes:

1. The method call `toUpperCase()` returns a string that has all characters in the original string converted to upper-case.

2. Likewise, the method call `toLowerCase()` can be used to return a string where all the characters of the original string have been converted to lower-case.

2.4.2 Locating a character within a string

Example 13

```
public class Pos
{
    public static void main(String [] args)
    {
        String name = "Tony Hawken";

        int i = name.indexOf('n');
        System.out.println("The first occurrence of n is at " +
                            "position " + i);

        int j = name.indexOf('n', i+1);
        System.out.println("The second occurrence of n is at " +
                            "position " + j);
```

```
        }
}
```

```
cmd

E:\JavaDev>java Pos
The first occurrence of n is at position 2
The second occurrence of n is at position 10

E:\JavaDev>_
```

Notes:

1. The method call `indexOf('n')` locates the first occurrence of the letter n, and returns its position in the string.

2. The method call `indexOf('n', i+1)` locates the first n after position i. That is, it is being used to locate the next occurrence of the letter n.

2.4.3 Comparison

`object.equals(s)`   returns true if s has the same value as the string within object

`object.compareTo(s)`   returns a positive number if the string is greater than s, 0 if they are equal, or a negative value if it is less than s.

This will be covered at a later date.

2.4.4   Replacing characters in a string

e.g   `name.replace('a', 'b');`   This method returns a String object with every occurrence of an 'a' replaced by a 'b'.

2.4.5 Converting primitive types to Strings

```
float pi = 3.142;
System.out.println("pi is printed as " + pi);

String piStr = String.valueOf(pi);
```

Notes:

Primitive data types can be converted to Strings

1. implicitly - concatenation ensures that pi is converted to an anonymous String object before it is printed using the `println()` method.

2. explicitly - the method `valueOf()` is called explicitly converting pi to a string before it is stored in the String object `piStr`.

2.5 Use of wrapper classes

The following program demonstrates how numerical data can be extracted from a String object. If you wish to perform arithmetic operations on data it must first be converted to the appropriate numerical type - in this case integer. To do this we have to use a wrapper class.

Example 14

```
public class string3
{
     public static void main(String[] args)
     {
          String MyBirthday = "22/05/1956";
          // Obtain substrings for day, month, year
          String Bday = MyBirthday.substring(0,2);
          String Bmonth = MyBirthday.substring(3,5);
          String Byear = MyBirthday.substring(6);

          // Convert substrings to integers
          int d = Integer.parseInt(Bday);
          int m = Integer.parseInt(Bmonth);
          int y = Integer.parseInt(Byear);

          // Output integer values
          System.out.println("Day = " + d);
          System.out.println("Month = " + m);
          System.out.println("Year = " + y);
     }
}
```

```
E:\JavaDev>java string3
Day = 22
Month = 5
Year = 1956
```

Notes:

1. Each of the primitive data-types boolean, char, byte, short, int, long, float, double have a **wrapper class** associated with them.

2. The wrapper classes are Boolean, Character, Byte, Short, Integer, Long, Float, Double.

3. The purpose of a **wrapper class** is to **encapsulate** or wrap-up a **primitive type** so that it can be used in the same way as an object.

4. **Integer** is a wrapper class for the data-type **int**. It contains methods such as parseInt() which are used to convert a **String** object to an **int**.

5. The other wrapper classes contain similar methods to convert a String object to that particular data-type.

Primitive data type	Wrapper class	Parse method
byte	Byte	parseByte()
short	Short	parseShort()
int	Integer	parseInteger()
float	Float	parseFloat()
double	Double	parseDouble()
boolean	Boolean	parseBoolean()

2.6   The Character class.

The Character class provides methods for manipulating characters. A small selection is included below. Most of those that follow are used to determine the type of a character - letter, digit, space, lowercase or uppercase etc. These always return a boolean. The last 3 examples are used to modify a character. These all return a char with the modified character.

equals(Object obj)   Compares the object with obj

isDefined(char ch)   returns true if ch is a valid unicode character

isDigit(char ch)   returns true if ch is a valid digit in the unicode character set

isLetter(char ch)   returns true if ch is a unicode letter

isLetterOrDigit(char ch)   returns true if ch is a unicode letter or digit

isLowerCase(char ch)   returns true if ch is a lowercase unicode character

isTitleCase(char ch)   returns true if ch is a titlecase character

isUpperCase(char ch)   returns true if ch is an uppercase character

isWhitespace(char ch)   returns true if ch is white space

toLowerCase(char ch)   returns the lowercase character corresponding to ch

toTitleCase(char ch)   returns the titlecase character corresponding to ch

```
toUpperCase(char ch)    returns the uppercase character corresponding to ch
```

Example 15

```
public class charDemo
{
    public static void main(String [] args)
    {
        char ch = 'a';

        System.out.println("Is character a digit ? " +
                        Character.isDigit(ch));
        System.out.println("Is character a letter ? " +
                        Character.isLetter(ch));
        System.out.println("Is character lowercase ? " +
                        Character.isLowerCase(ch));
        System.out.println("Is character uppercase ? " +
                        Character.isUpperCase(ch));
        System.out.println("Converted to uppercase, the" +
                        "character is : " +
                        Character.toUpperCase(ch));
    }
}
```

```
cmd

E:\JavaDev>java charDemo
Is character a digit ? false
Is character a letter ? true
Is character lowercase ? true
Is character uppercase ? false
Converted to uppercase, the character is : A

E:\JavaDev>_
```

Notes:

In this example program we are displaying the value returned by the method called. The first 4 methods return a boolean – true or false. In the case of the last method the upper-case character is returned.

36

Exercise 2-1

1. Write a program that will extract items of data from a string. Your program will contain the following statements:

```
String book1, book2;
book1 = "1445243407/Tony Hawken/A C++ Notebook/13.95";
book2 = "1445724243/Tony Hawken/A web Notebook/15.00";
```

The program will then use a number of string methods to extract the 4 sub-strings separated by the separator '/'.

Using the string book1 as an example, they should be displayed as follows:

```
Book1
ISBN:      1445243407
Author:    Tony Hawken
Title:     A C++ Notebook
Price:     13.95
```

2. Redo the above question. This time when you extract the sub-strings, convert them to an appropriate data-type as follows.

Sub-string	data-type
ISBN	long int
Author	String
Title	String
Price	double

Add statements to your program so that the ISBN is incremented by one, and the price of the book is displayed in dollars. Use the following for carrying out the conversion: 1 British pound = 1.54 U.S. dollars

For book 1 your output should look something like this:

```
The next available ISBN is 1445243408
The price in dollars is 21.483
```

2.7 The Scanner class and console input

There are many different ways in which you can obtain keyboard input in your programs using Java. It is for this reason, that the AP (Advanced placement) programme for computer science does not test keyboard input. Up until recently (Java 5) keyboard input was horrendously complicated. When I was using Java around 10 years ago, the books that I had, often introduced keyboard input near the end of the book. This changed with the introduction of the Scanner class which greatly simplifies keyboard input.

The scanner class allows you to input different data types from different sources. In the examples that I will give, the source of input will always be the keyboard. This is associated with the object System.in.

The following example program, is a modified version of an earlier program with keyboard input added.

Example 16

```
// Convert Centigrade to Fahrenheit

import java.util.Scanner;

public class temp2
{
     public static void main(String [] args)
     {

          Scanner input = new Scanner(System.in);

          System.out.print("Enter a temperature in degrees C : ");
          float c = input.nextFloat();

          float f = 9/5 * c + 32;

          System.out.print("C = " + c);
          System.out.println("\t F = " + f);
     }
}
```

```
C:\ cmd

E:\JavaDev>java temp2
Enter a temperature in degrees C : 25
C = 25.0          F = 57.0
```

Notes:

1. A new Scanner object called input is created when you execute the statement:

```
Scanner input = new Scanner(System.in);
```

2. The parameter System.in ties the input to the keyboard.

3. The method `nextFloat()` is called by the input object. This method returns a float. If an integer is entered instead, this will be converted to a float.

4. In the example run shown, I entered a value of 25. This is converted to a value of 25.0 – as c is a float.

2.8   Methods in the Scanner class

In this section we will look at some of the methods available within the scanner class. In particular we wish to be able to extract different types of data from the standard input stream (keyboard)

Example 17

```java
import java.util.Scanner;

public class kbInput
{
    public static void main(String args[])
    {
        Scanner input = new Scanner(System.in);

        System.out.print("Enter a string :");
        String st = input.nextLine();
        System.out.print("Enter a byte : ");
        byte b = input.nextByte();
        System.out.print("Enter a short : ");
        short s = input.nextShort();
        System.out.print("Enter an int : ");
        int i = input.nextInt();
        System.out.print("Enter a long : ");
        long l = input.nextLong();
        System.out.print("Enter a float : ");
        float f = input.nextFloat();
        System.out.print("Enter a double : ");
        double d = input.nextDouble();


        System.out.print("The data entered is : ");
        System.out.print(b + "   " + s + "   " + i + "   ");
        System.out.print(l + "   " + f + "   " + d + "   ");
        System.out.println(st);
    }
}
```

```
cmd

E:\JavaDev>java kbInput
Enter a string :Tony Hawken
Enter a byte : 3
Enter a short : 123
Enter an int : 12345
Enter a long : 1234567
Enter a float : 12.75
Enter a double : 12.1234
The data entered is : 3   123   12345   1234567   12.75   12.1234   Tony Hawken

E:\JavaDev>_
```

Notes:

1. The method `nextLine()` all of the input entered up until a return was pressed. These characters are returned as a character string.

2. The method `nextByte()` returns a byte.

3. The method `nextShort()` returns a short.

4. The method `nextInt()` returns an int.

5. The method `nextLong()` returns a long.

6. The method `nextFloat()` returns a float.

7. The method `nextDouble()` returns a double.

8. You would expect there to be a method called `nextChar()` that will return a char. But, unfortunately it doesn't exist. As far as I know, there is no such method that will return a char.

9. You can get round this problem using the following fudge.

```
String s = input.nextLine();
Char c = s.charAt(0);
```

10. The method call `s.charAt(0)` will return the first character from the string s. This is not really satisfactory as a user may enter a whitespace character.

2.9　　Solving quadratic equations

A quadratic equation is an equation of the form $ax^2 + bx + c = 0$

it can be solved with the formula:

$$x = \frac{-b \pm \sqrt{b^2 - 4ac}}{2a}$$

this provides us with two solutions

$$x1 = \frac{-b + \sqrt{b^2 - 4ac}}{2a} \qquad \text{and} \qquad x2 = \frac{-b - \sqrt{b^2 - 4ac}}{2a}$$

To code this in Java, we need to input 3 numbers from the keyboard. We then need to do a couple of calculations before displaying the results on the screen.

Example 18

```java
import java.util.Scanner;

public class quad
{
   public static void main(String [] args)
   {
     int a, b, c;    //3 quadratic coefficients

     Scanner input = new Scanner(System.in);

     System.out.print("Enter 3 coefficients a, b, c: ");
     a = input.nextInt();
     b = input.nextInt();
     c = input.nextInt();

     double d = (double) (b * b - 4 * a * c);
     double d2 = Math.sqrt(d);
     double x1 = (-b + d) / (2 * a);
     double x2 = (-b - d) / (2 * a);

     System.out.println("x is either " + x1 + " or " + x2);
     }
}
```

```
cmd

E:\JavaDev>java quad
Enter 3 coefficients a, b, c: 1 -12 16
x is either 46.0 or -34.0

E:\JavaDev>java quad
Enter 3 coefficients a, b, c: 3 -7 11
x is either -12.66666666666666 or 15.0
```

Notes:

1. The variables a, b and c are used to store 3 integers entered at the keyboard.

2. These integer values can be entered on the same line provided they are separated by whitespace. That is, they are separated by one or more spaces or tabs.

3. The formula for a quadratic equation is worked out in parts. This means that that part of the calculation is only done once. It also simplifies the expressions.

4. The **Math** class provides us with the `sqrt()` method that enables us to calculate square roots.

2.10   Formatted output

You can format output using a `printf` statement. This has the format:

```
System.out.printf(formatString, listOfArguments);
```

Here formatString is like a string in a println statement, except that it includes special characters called format specifiers. All format specifiers begin with the character %. These format specifiers mark the position within the string where the next data item from the list of arguments will appear. They also specify how that data item will be displayed.

We could improve the previous program by formatting the output – in this case specify the number of decimal places. This can be achieved by replacing the `println` statement with the following `printf` statement.

```
System.out.printf("x is either %.2f or %.2f \n", x1, x2);
```

```
cmd

E:\JavaDev>java quad2
Enter 3 coefficients a, b, c: 3 -7 11
x is either -12.67 or 15.00

E:\JavaDev>_
```

Notes:

1. The format string within the printf statement contains two format specifiers. They are used to format the output of x1 and x2 correct to 2 decimal places.

2. The following format specifiers are available:

s – string, c – unicode character, d – decimal integer, e – floating point number in scientific notation, f – floating point number(usual format).

2.11   Use of numeric constants and scientific notation

Newton's law of gravitation states that the force of attraction between two bodes is directly proportional to the masses of the two bodies and inversely proportional to the distance between them.

This can be described more succinctly with the equation $F = \dfrac{GMm}{r^2}$

Where G is the gravitational constant, M and m are the masses of the two bodies, and d is the distance between them, and F the attractive force. In this example the bodies are the Sun and Earth.

Here   M = 1.9889×10^{30} Kg = mass of the Sun
m = 5.9742×10^{24} Kg = mass of the Earth
d = 1.4940×10^{11} m   = distance between the Sun and the Earth
G = 6.6730×10^{-11} Nm^2Kg^{-2} = The universal gravitational constant
F = force of attraction in Newtons (N)

You will notice that we are using both very large and very small numbers. These numbers are expressed in standard form or scientific notation and are stored as constants. The answer generated from the calculation is going to be very large, so it is important to format it appropriately – using scientific notation.

Example 19

```
public class g
{
    public static void main( String [] args)
    {
        //Numeric constants
        final double M = 1.9889e+30; //Mass of Sun in Kg
        final double m = 5.9742e+24; //Mass of Earth in Kg
        final double d = 1.4940e+11; //distance between them
        final double G = 6.6730e-11; //gravitational constant

        //Calculation
        double F = G*M*m/(d*d);

        System.out.printf("The force F = %.4e N\n", F);
    }
}
```

```
c:\ cmd

E:\JavaDev>java g
The force F = 3.5523e+22 N

E:\JavaDev>
```

43

Notes:

1. The keyword final states that for a given variable the initialized value cannot be changed. In other words, the variable is a constant.

2. Using constants in the manner makes the program safer as it is impossible for them to be changed when the program runs. Also, use of named constants in this manner makes the program easier to understand and maintain.

3. The format specifier `%.4e` is used to format the output using scientific notation and to 4 decimal places.

2.12   The Math class revisited

So far we have used the method `sqrt()` to evaluate square roots. The Math class provides a number of essential mathematical methods (functions) and a couple of important mathematical constants. Here, we will be looking at those that you are likely to have seen before, and can be found on your calculator.

Trigonometric functions

`sin()`, `cos()` and `tan()`. These all have a single parameter of type double – the angle in radians. They return the trigonometric ratio (double). As a reminder, I have included a diagram to represent the trigonometric ratios.

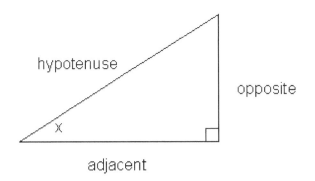

$$\sin x = \frac{\text{opposite}}{\text{hypotenuse}} \qquad \cos x = \frac{\text{adjacent}}{\text{hypotenuse}} \qquad \tan x = \frac{\text{opposite}}{\text{adjacent}}$$

You can convert angles in degrees to radians using the following formula.

2π Radians = 360 degrees.

Inverse trigonometric functions

The methods `asin()`, `acos()` and `atan()` have a single parameter a trigonometric ratio of type double. They return a value of type double – the angle measured in radians. On your calculator these methods will appear as $\sin^{-1}$, $\cos^{-1}$ and $\tan^{-1}$.

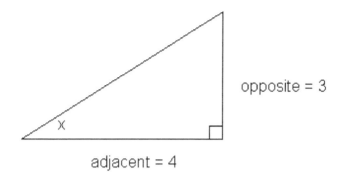

$$\tan x = \frac{\text{opposite}}{\text{adjacent}} = \frac{3}{4} = 0.75 \Rightarrow x = \tan^{-1} x$$

Powers, roots and logarithms

The `sqrt()` method has a single parameter of type double – the number whose square root you wish to evaluate. It returns a single value – the positive square root of the number (double).

The `pow()` method is an exponential function. It is declared as:

```
static double pow( double x, double y)
```

It is used to evaluate x^y (x to the power of y) You could however use the `pow()` method to calculate square roots. This can be achieved by setting y = 0.5.

The `exp()` method is also an exponential function. It is used to calculate e^x (e to the power of x).

The `log()` method returns the logarithm of a number to base e. That is, it is an inverse function to the `exp()` function.

Numeric constants

The following important numeric constants are available in the Math class.

```
Math.PI = 3.141592658979323846
```

```
Math.E = 2.7182818284590452354
```

Exercise 2-2

1. Simple interest paid on a sum invested in a bank is given by the formula:

   I = PRT/100   P = sum of money invested   R = rate of interest (%)
                         T = time saved in years   I = interest gained (£)

   Write a program that will allow the user to enter values for P, R and T and will then compute and print out the simple interest.

2. Write a program that allows the user to enter a 4-digit integer. The program will then use a quotient and remainder technique to extract each of the digits. These are to be stored in the variables d1, d2, d3 and d4. You should demonstrate that the program works correctly by displaying the values of d1, d2, d3 and d4.

   For the number n = 6539   d1 = 6, d2 = 5, d3 = 3, d4 = 9.
   Use   n / 1000   to extract the thousands digit
   Use   n % 1000 to get the remainder.

3. Einstein's most famous equation is $E = mc^2$. This calculates an amount of energy in Joules given a loss in mass (m) in Kg. It uses the speed of light (c).

   Given that the speed of light is 299,792,500 ms^{-1}, write a program that calculates and prints out E for a given value of m input at the keyboard. Represent c as a numeric constant. Choose appropriate data types.

4. Write a program that can calculate the area of any triangle, given the lengths of the 3 sides. Use the information below.

   Heron's formula can be used to calculate the area of any triangle.

   $$\text{Area} = \sqrt{s(s-a)(s-b)(s-c)} \quad \text{where } s = \frac{(a+b+c)}{2}$$

5. Write a program to work out a person's change. It is assumed that the item costs less than £10 and that the person only has a £10 note to pay with. The required change should then be calculated so that a minimum number of coins are given. No notes are given as change.

   Analysis of problem

   1. Easier if change is converted to pence.
   2. Coins currently available are £2, £1, 50p, 20p, 10p, 5p, 2p, 1p.
   3. Need to keep a coin count for each coin.
   4. Can use the built-in arithmetic operators / and %.

Week 3

Control structures

3.1 Comparison and Logical operators

When making decisions and for performing repetition we often require the following operators. They are the same as in C or C++.

<	less than
<=	less than or equal
>	greater than
>=	greater than or equal
==	equal to
!=	not equal to

- The operators <, <=, >, >= are known as relational operators, whereas the operators == and != are called equality operators.

- We can use these operators to form simple **Boolean** expressions - which evaluate to either true or false. They can be used with all primitive data types.

- Compound Boolean expressions can be formed by joining two or more simple expressions with logical operators.

Example 20

```
// Demonstrate use of boolean expressions
public class bool
{
    public static void main(String [] args)
    {
        int a = 1, b = 2, c = 3, d = 4;
        System.out.println(a == 1);
        System.out.println(b != 2);
        System.out.println(a >= 1 && b < 4);
        System.out.println(c <= 6 && b < c);
    }
}
```

```
E:\JavaDev>java bool
true
false
true
true
```

3.1.1   Logical operators

Logical operators are used to combine 2 or more Boolean statements.

operator	name	example	interpretation
&&	Logical AND	a && b	true if both a and b are true
||	Logical OR	a || b	true if either a or b or both are true
!	NOT	!a	true if a is false and vis versa

The following truth tables summarise the properties of &&, || and ! explicitly.

&& (AND)

x	y	x && y
false	false	false
true	false	false
false	true	false
true	true	true

|| (OR)

x	y	x || y
false	false	false
true	false	true
false	true	true
true	true	true

! (NOT)

x	! x
false	true
true	false

Exercise 3-1

1.   Some examples of Boolean expressions follow:

(a)   5 == 7

(b)   9 <= 9

(c)   11 > 14 - 5

(d)   (15 > 5) || (7 == 0)

(e)   (15 > 5) && (7 == 0)

(f)   !(15 > 5) || !(7 == 0)

(g)   !(15 > 5) && (7 == 0)

(h)   !((15 > 5) && (7 == 0))

For each of the 8 expressions above determine whether they evaluate true or false. You could consider writing a program to compute the results.

3.2   The if statement

The if statement in java is the same as in C and C++.

The simplest format is:

```
if (expression) statement;
```

This is interpreted as "if the expression is true, execute the statement, otherwise do nothing". An example follows :-

```
if (num > 0)
    System.out.println("number is positive");
```

This can be extended to provide an action should the expression evaluate false.

```
if (num > 0)
    System.out.println("number is positive");
else
    System.out.println("number is not positive");
```

This example can be taken a stage further, after all we really want to be able to say the number is positive, negative or zero.

```
if (num > 0)
    System.out.println("number is positive");
else if (num < 0)
    System.out.println("number is negative");
else
    System.out.println("number is zero");
```

This last example is often called a multi-way if statement, and in Computer Science this is called a **case** structure. In many situations this can be re-coded using a **switch** statement, which follows later.

Often when using an **if** statement you will want to execute several statements should a condition be true. This can be achieved by using a **compound statement**, or **block**. You can use a statement block anywhere in the program where you could insert a single statement.

A program that demonstrates the if statement simply follows.

Example 21

```java
import java.util.Scanner;

public class if1
{
    public static void main(String [] args)
    {
        int n;
        Scanner num = new Scanner(System.in);

        System.out.print("Enter a number :");
        n = num.nextInt();

        if (n > 0)
            System.out.println("number is positive");
        else if (n < 0)
            System.out.println("number is negative");
        else
            System.out.println("number is zero");
    }
}
```

Notes:

1. The Scanner class is used to create a Scanner object called num. This is used to extract an integer using the method `nextInt()`.

2. For the integer obtained, there are three possibilities. The number is greater than 0 (positive), less than 0 (negative), and if it is not one of the first two, it must be zero.

3.3 Compute a leap year

A leap year can be determined by following the rules below:

(a) Write a program that will accept a given year. The program will then determine whether this year is a leap year and print an appropriate message. You may consider using the following rules for determining leap years.

- The year is divisible by 4 but not by 100
- The year is divisible by 4 and by 400

(b) Continue this program by allowing a user to enter a number that represents a month. Given this month and the fact that the year is a leap year, or not a leap year will work out how many days in the month.

Example 22

```java
import java.util.Scanner;

public class leapyr
{
    public static void main(String [] args)
    {
        int days, y, m;
        boolean leapyear;

        Scanner input = new Scanner(System.in);
        System.out.print("Enter a year : ");
        y = input.nextInt();


        if((y % 4 == 0 && y % 100 != 0) ||
           (y % 4 == 0 && y % 400 == 0))
        {
            leapyear = true;
            System.out.println("Year " + y + " is a leapyear");
        }
        else
        {
            leapyear = false;
            System.out.println("Year " + y + " is not a leapyear");
        }

        System.out.print("Enter month (1-12): ");
        m = input.nextInt();

        if (m == 4 || m == 6 || m == 9 || m == 11)
            days = 30;
        else if (m == 1 || m == 3 || m == 5 || m == 7 || m == 8
                    || m == 10 || m == 12)
            days = 31;
        else
```

```
        {
            if (!leapyear)
                days = 28;
            else
                days = 29;
        }

        System.out.println("There are " + days +
                            " days in the month ");
    }
}
```

```
E:\JavaDev>java leapyr
Enter a year : 2010
Year 2010 is not a leapyear
Enter month (1-12): 2
There are 28 days in the month
```

Notes:

1. The expression   y % 4 == 0 && y % 100 != 0   is used to determine whether the year is divisible by 4, but not divisible by 100.

2. The expression   y % 4 == 0 && y % 400 == 0   is used to determine whether the year is divisible by 4 and divisible by 400. Is this really necessary?

3. If either of these expressions evaluates true, then a variable called leapyr is set to true. This can be used later when we want to determine the number of days in February.

4. There are 30 days in September, April, June and November. All the other months have 31 except for February that has 28 for a non-leap year and 29 for a leap year.

3.4   The switch statement

The switch statement in Java is a very primitive implementation of a case structure. It provides a very limited form of multi-way selection. The following code has been taken from the previous program and re-coded. The if statement used to determine the number of days in a month has now been rewritten as a switch statement.

Example 23

```
switch(m)
{ case 4:
  case 6:
  case 9:
  case 11: days = 30;
            break;
       case 1:
       case 3:
  case 5:
  case 7:
  case 8:
  case 12: days = 31;
            break;
  case 2:  if (leapyear == false)
                days = 28;
            else
                days = 29;
            break;
  default: System.out.println("Invalid month entered");
}
```

Notes:

1. The variable m must be of integral type. i.e. byte, char, short, int or long.

2. The value of m is compared with each of the case labels.

3. If there is a match, the statements associated with the label are executed.

4. In the above example if m is either 4, 6, 9 or 11, days is assigned the value 31.

5. The break statement is needed to exit the switch statement.

6. The default label will match any value not mentioned previously in the case labels.

3.5   The ternary operator

The ternary operator, or conditional operator has a similar job to the if statement but it is more flexible because it can be included in other statements where an expression can reside such as a `System.out.println` statement.

It has the form:

```
expression1 ? expression2 : expression3
```

In this case, `expression1` is evaluated to determine whether `expression2` or `expression3` is to be used. If `expresion1` evaluates true, then `expression2` will be run, otherwise `expression3`.

Using an if statement we could write:

```
if (x < 0)
    System.out.println("The sign of  " + x + " is positive");
else
    System.out.println("The sign of " + x + " is negative");
```

This can be simplified using the ternary operator to:

```
System.out.println("The sign of " + x + " is " + (x > y ?
"positive" : "negative"));
```

We could also use the ternary operator to determine the largest number

Instead of writing:

```
if(a > b)
    max = a;
else
    max = b;
```

we could write:

```
max = (a > b ? a : b);
```

This could be extended to cope with 3 numbers by nesting within the conditional statement as follows:

```
max = (a > b ? (a > c ? a : c) : (b > c ? b : c));
```

Exercise 3-2

1. (a) Write a program that will prompt a user to enter a number between 1 and 100

    (b) Test the number input to see if it is:

    (i)   even
    (ii) odd
    (iii) greater than 50

    (c) Print appropriate responses for each of these tests.

2. Write a short program that will prompt a user for an exam mark in the range 1-100 and will respond by printing the mark and grade.

    The rules for awarding grades are as follows:

mark	grade
79 - 100	A
67 - 78	B
54 - 66	C
40 - 53	D
< 40	F

3. Write a program that will input a person's height in centimetres (cm), and weight in kilograms (kg). The output from the program will be one of the following messages: underweight, normal, or overweight, using the criteria:

    Underweight: weight < height / 2.5
    Normal: height / 2.5 ≤ weight ≤ height / 2.3
    Overweight: height/ 2.3 < weight

4. Modify the previous program used to calculate the roots of quadratic equations so that it will check that the solution has real roots. Otherwise display "Equation has no real roots". (Note – for real solutions $b^2 > 4ac$).

5. Write a program that will input 3 names from the keyboard. The program will then display the 3 names in alphabetical order.

3.6   Validation and verification

Selection can be usefully employed to check input data. There are two main ways to check input data. **Validation** and **verification**.

Validation is the process of the program checking that the data input and so likely to be correct. The following is an example.

3.6.1   Validation

The following program illustrates a range check. This is a simple type of validation in which you check whether a numeric value is between two values.

Example 24

```java
import java.util.Scanner;

public class range
{
   public static void main(String [] args)

   {
     int n;     //number to check

     Scanner input = new Scanner(System.in);

     System.out.print("Enter a number between 1 and 10 : ");

     n = input.nextInt();

     // Perform a range check
     if(n >= 1 && n <= 10)
          System.out.println("Valid data entered");
     else
          System.out.println("Invalid data entered");
   }
}
```

```
E:\JavaDev>java range
Enter a number between 1 and 10 : 11
Invalid data entered

E:\JavaDev>java range
Enter a number between 1 and 10 : 7
Valid data entered
```

Note:

This example uses a range check to see if the number entered is between 1 and 10. If the value is within this range it is deemed to be valid.

3.6.2   Length of a string

Here is another example. This time a check on the length of a string is used.

<u>Example 25</u>

```java
import java.util.Scanner;

public class strlength
{
    public static void main(String [] args)
    {
      String name;

      Scanner input = new Scanner(System.in);

      System.out.print("Enter a name (10 characters) : ");
      name = input.nextLine();

      if (name.length() > 10)
      {
          System.out.println("Name is too long");
          System.out.println("truncation will occur");
          String name2 = name.substring(0,10);
          System.out.println("Truncated name = " + name2);
      }
      else
      {
          System.out.println("Name doesn't exceed 10 characters");
          System.out.println("name = " + name);
      }
    }
}
```

```
C:\ cmd

E:\JavaDev>java strlength
Enter a name (10 characters) : Encyclopaedia
Name is too long
truncation will occur
Truncated name = Encyclopae
```

Note:

1. The method `length()` returns the length of a string.

2. `substring()` is used to truncate a String object that is too long. In this case the first 10 characters are extracted.

3.6.3   Verification

A common technique to check that a user has not mistyped their password is to make them enter the same password twice. This example uses the `equals()` method to test the equality of two strings.

Example 26

```java
import java.util.Scanner;

public class pwd
{
   public static void main(String [] args)
   {
     String password1, password2;

     Scanner input = new Scanner(System.in);

     System.out.print("Enter new password : ");
     password1 = input.nextLine();

     System.out.print("verification - enter password again : ");
     password2 = input.nextLine();

     if (password1.equals(password2))
     {
         System.out.println("Password being changed");
         String password = new String(password1);
     }
     else
     {
         System.out.print("Verification error ");
         System.out.println("- password not changed");
     }
   }
}
```

```
cmd

E:\JavaDev>java pwd
Enter new password : awkward
verification - enter password again : awkward
Password being changed
```

Notes:

1. The String method `equals()` is used to compare two passwords. You cannot use the operator == to compare strings, as strings are objects.

2. When you use the `equals()` method you are comparing the values stored in the two strings.

3. If you do use the == operator to compare strings, you are actually comparing a reference to the two objects. That is you are testing whether the two object are the same.

4. An alternative to having to type the data twice, and let the program check the two data items, is to display the input data and let the user check it. This will be left as an exercise later.

3.7 Comparing two strings

In the two programs that follow, we will be using the method compareTo() to compare strings. In the program that follows it will be demonstrated that the method compareTo() returns a numeric value, and that this value can be used to order the strings alphabetically.

Example 27

```
public class CompareWords
{
    public static void main(String [] args)
    {
        String w1 = "byte";
        String w2 = "Byte";
        String w3 = "bite";
        String w4 = "bitten";

        System.out.println("compare w1 with w2 gives " +
                        w1.compareTo(w2));
        System.out.println("compare w1 with w3 gives " +
                        w1.compareTo(w3));
        System.out.println("compare w1 with w4 gives " +
                        w1.compareTo(w4));
        System.out.println("compare w2 with w1 gives " +
                        w2.compareTo(w1));
        System.out.println("compare w2 with w2 gives " +
                        w2.compareTo(w2));
        System.out.println("compare w2 with w3 gives " +
                        w2.compareTo(w3));
    }
}
```

```
cmd

E:\JavaDev>java CompareWords
compare w1 with w2 gives 32
compare w1 with w3 gives 16
compare w1 with w4 gives 16
compare w2 with w1 gives -32
compare w2 with w2 gives 0
compare w2 with w3 gives -32

E:\JavaDev>_
```

Notes:

1. For the expression `str1.compareTo(str2)`, The String object str1 calls the method `compareTo()` with a parameter str2. This compares the values of the two strings str1 and str2.

2. If a negative value is returned, this indicates that str1 < str2. That is str1 comes before str2 alphabetically.

3. If a positive value is returned, this indicates that str1 > str2. That is str1 comes after str2 alphabetically.

4. If zero is returned, this indicates that the two strings are identical.

5. You must remember that these comparisons are case sensitive, and that alphabetical order is determined by how characters are ordered according to their Unicode representation.

6. A small sample of character codes are included here.

		codes
Numeric characters	0 - 9	48 - 57
Uppercase characters	A - Z	65 - 90
Lowercase characters	a - z	97 - 122

7. As well as punctuation characters, various non-printing characters and also some graphics characters are present.

8. So we could write the following valid expressions:

> **"a" < "b"**   Each of these can be verified by checking the table above
> **"Z" < "a"**
> **"4" < "6"**

9. Two strings are ordered by comparing their characters one at a time until there is a mismatch. Consider the following:

> "business" < "busy"

10. This can be represented as:

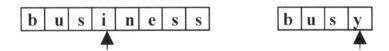

11. Here the first mismatch is at character position 4 indicating that "business" < "busy". In the same way if we consider the comparison of:

> **"word" < "words"**

The example program below, is a more realistic use of the `compareTo()` method.

Example 28

```java
import java.util.Scanner;

public class CompareWords2
{
    public static void main(String [] args)
    {
        String word1 = "Encyclopaedia";
        String word2;

        Scanner input = new Scanner(System.in);

        System.out.print("Enter your password : ");
        word2 = input.nextLine();

        if(word1.compareTo(word2) == 0)
            System.out.println(word2 + " is the same as " +
                                word1);
        else if (word1.compareTo(word2) < 0)
            System.out.println(word2 + " comes before " +
                                word1);
        else if (word1.compareTo(word2) > 0)
            System.out.println(word2 + " comes after " +
                                word1);
    }
}
```

```
cmd

E:\JavaDev>java CompareWords2
Enter your password : Encyclopaedia
Encyclopaedia is the same as Encyclopaedia

E:\JavaDev>java CompareWords2
Enter your password : encyclopaedia
encyclopaedia comes before Encyclopaedia

E:\JavaDev>_
```

Notes:

1. If the return value of `compareTo(word2)` is equal to zero, then the strings must match.

2. If the return value of `compareTo(word2)` is a negative number (less than 0) then the word entered must alphabetically come before word 1.

3. If the return value of `compareTo(word2)` is a positive number (greater than 0) then the word entered must alphabetically come after word 1.

Exercise 3-3

1. Write a program to demonstrate a user checking the input data

(a) The program should allow a user to enter their name and address. Their address consists of address line1, address line 2, address line 3.

(b) The details entered will then be displayed on the screen, and the user will be asked if these details are correct. They should reply with a y for yes, or n for no.

(c) If y is entered, a message should be displayed, that the data is being processed and if an n has been entered, a message indicating that a verification error has occurred.

3.8 Iteration

There are many programming problems that require the same sequence of statements to be executed again and again, either a fixed number of times or an indefinite number of times. One way to do this would be to type in the same code many times. However, this is very impractical, especially if the code needs to be repeated many times. Also, we don't always know in advance how many times the statements are to be repeated.

Iteration is another word for repetition or looping. Rather than repeat the same statements many times it makes more sense to have a control structure specify that certain statements are to be repeated. In Java as in the C and C++ there are 3 main control statements - **for**, **while** and **do ... while** statements. The syntax is the same in all 3 languages.

3.9 The for statement

The following example program uses a for loop to enter 5 numbers, and add these numbers to a total. The average can then be determined by dividing by 5.

Example 29

```java
//Compute the average of 5 numbers input from keyboard

import java.util.Scanner;

public class for1
{
    public static void main(String [] args)
    {
      double n, total = 0.0;

      Scanner input = new Scanner(System.in);

      for(int c = 1; c <= 5; c++)
      {
          System.out.print("Enter next number : ");
          n = input.nextDouble();

          total += n;
      }
      double average = total / 5;
      System.out.println("The average value is " + average);
    }
}
```

```
E:\JavaDev>java for1
Enter next number : 5.4
Enter next number : 3.2
Enter next number : 8.7
Enter next number : 4.9
Enter next number : 1.5
The average value is 4.74
```

Notes:

1. The for statement has the general format:

   ```
   for (expr1, expr2, expr3) statement;
   ```

2. expr1 - `int c = 1`. This creates an integer called c and initializes it with the value 1.

3. c is called a control variable or counter

4. `expr2 - c <= 5`. This test is used to determine how many times the code is to be repeated. It is applied at the beginning of the loop.

5. `expr3 - c++`. This is the final action and needs to be performed to increment the counter

6. statement can be a single statement, or a compound statement. In the above example a compound statement is used.

7. The for statement is generally only used when statements need to be repeated a fixed number of times.

8. The statement `total += n;` is equivalent to `total = total + n;`. It is used to add n to the current total.

3.10   The while statement

<u>Example 30</u>

```java
// Compute average of 5 numbers entered at the keyboard

import java.util.Scanner;

public class while1
{
    public static void main(String [] args)
    {
      double n, total = 0.0;

      Scanner input = new Scanner(System.in);

      int c = 1;
      while (c <= 5)
      {
            System.out.print("Enter next number : ");
            n = input.nextDouble();

            total += n;
            c++;
      }
      double average = total / 5;
      System.out.println("The average value is " + average);
    }
}
```

Notes:

1. The **while** statement is really a general purpose **for** statement.

2. The **control variable** c is initialised before the start of the while loop.

3. The general format of a while loop is:

   ```
   while(expression) statement;
   ```

4. When the expression evaluates true the loop terminates.

5. The control variable c needs to be incremented within the while loop.

6. If the same numbers are entered, the output is the same as for the previous program.

3.11   The do ... while statement

<u>Example 31</u>

```java
// Compute average of 5 numbers entered at the keyboard

import java.util.Scanner;

public class do1
{
   public static void main(String [] args)
   {

      double n, total = 0.0;

      Scanner input = new Scanner(System.in);

      int c = 1;
      do
      {
           System.out.print("Enter next number : ");
           n = input.nextDouble();
           total += n;
           c++;
      }
      while (c <= 5);
      double average = total / 5;
      System.out.println("The average value is " + average);
   }
}
```

Notes:

The test is applied last in a **do ... while** loop.

3.12 Using the control variable in a calculation

Example 32

```java
// Compute and print out a multiplication table

import java.util.Scanner;

public class for2

{
   public static void main(String [] args)
   {
     Scanner input = new Scanner(System.in);

     System.out.print("Enter number : ");
     int n = input.nextInt();

     for(int c = 1; c <= 10; c++)
         System.out.println(c + " * " + n + " = " + c * n);

   }
}
```

Note:

The control variable c is used as part of a calculation. That it is displayed to indicate the number of the iteration, also it is used to compute the product.

Exercise 3-4

1. Write a program, which will allow you to enter you name and then print it 20 times on the screen. Experiment by using both the `print()` and `println()` methods.

2. Write 2 versions of a program to convert Centigrade to Fahrenheit

(a) so that the temperature in degrees Centigrade takes integer values in the range 1 to 20.
(b) so that the temperature in degrees Centigrade takes integer values in the range 0 to 100 and also goes up by 10 each time.

3. Write a program which will calculate factorials - given that 5 factorial can be obtained using the expression $5 \times 4 \times 3 \times 2 \times 1$.

(a) What is the largest factorial you can obtain using your factorial program. Try experimenting with different numeric data-types.
(b) Rewrite the program using a while loop.

4. Leonhard Euler first pointed out that the formula $x^2 - x + 41$ can be used to generate prime numbers for all values of x between 1 and 40. Write a program to demonstrate this.

5. A number is prime if it has exactly two factors, 1 and itself. So 1 is not a prime number as the only divisor is 1. However 2, 3 and 5 are as each has exactly two factors.

You can test for a prime number using the remainder operator (%). If you divide the number by another number and the remainder is zero, you know that that number is a factor.

Write a program that will display all the prime numbers between 1 and 100.

3.13   Repeating a variable number of times

<u>Example 33</u>

```java
// Compute average of a set of numbers terminated by -1

import java.util.Scanner;

public class varloop
{
   public static void main(String [] args)
   {
     Scanner input = new Scanner(System.in);

     System.out.println("Enter a set of numbers" +
                        "terminated by -1");

     int c = 0;
     double n = 0.0, total = 0.0;
     while (n != -1)
     {
         System.out.print("Enter next number : ");
         n = input.nextDouble();

         if (n != -1) { total += n; c++; }
     }
     double average = total / c;
     System.out.println("The average value is " + average);
   }
}
```

```
C:\ cmd

E:\JavaDev>java varloop
Enter a set of numbers terminated by -1
Enter next number : 6.8
Enter next number : 3.7
Enter next number : 4.6
Enter next number : 3
Enter next number : -1
The average value is 4.525
```

Notes:

1. The value -1 is being used as a data terminator; it is not a valid data item, it is merely included to terminate input.

2. To check that the data-terminator is not included in the calculation, an if statement is used to check whether the current number is a valid number for the calculation.

3.14   Using a break to terminate a loop

The following problem is used to demonstrate another technique for repetition.

The equation $x^3 + x = 11$ has a solution slightly greater than 2. Find the solution to 2 decimal places by calculating $y = x^3 + x$ for values of x increasing in steps of 0.01 from x = 2, stopping when y first exceeds 11.

Example 34

```java
public class numericalSol
{
    public static void main(String [] args)
    {
        double x = 2.0, y;
        for(; ; )
        {
            y = x * x * x + x;
            System.out.println("When x = " + x + "\ty = " + y);

            if (y >= 11)
                break;
            else
                x += 0.01;
        }
    }
}
```

```
c:\ cmd

E:\JavaDev>java numericalSol
When x = 2.0        y = 10.0
When x = 2.01       y = 10.130600999999997
When x = 2.0199999999999996      y = 10.262407999999994
When x = 2.0299999999999994      y = 10.39542699999999
When x = 2.0399999999999999      y = 10.529663999999988
When x = 2.0499999999999999      y = 10.665124999999986
When x = 2.0599999999999987      y = 10.801815999999983
When x = 2.0699999999999985      y = 10.93974299999998
When x = 2.0799999999999983      y = 11.078911999999976

E:\JavaDev>_
```

Notes:

6. The for loop used would cause an infinite loop if there where no break statements to exit from the loop.

7. An if statement checks when the value of y exceeds 11. When this occurs, a break statement is used to terminate the loop.

8. If the value of y is less than 11, x is incremented and the evaluation of y is repeated.

9. The output for this program is particularly messy. This is because the you get representation errors for floating point numbers when you add 0.01 on each time.

This program has been rewritten using a printf statement to overcome these problems.

Example 35

```java
public class numericalSol2
{
    public static void main(String [] args)
    {
        double x = 2.0, y;
        for(; ; )
        {
            y = x * x * x + x;
            System.out.printf("When x = %.2f\ty = %.4f\n", x, y );

            if (y >= 11)
                break;
            else
                x += 0.01;
        }
    }
}
```

```
C:\ cmd

E:\JavaDev>java numericalSol2
When x = 2.00    y = 10.0000
When x = 2.01    y = 10.1306
When x = 2.02    y = 10.2624
When x = 2.03    y = 10.3954
When x = 2.04    y = 10.5297
When x = 2.05    y = 10.6651
When x = 2.06    y = 10.8018
When x = 2.07    y = 10.9397
When x = 2.08    y = 11.0789

E:\JavaDev>
```

Notes:

1. The format string within the printf statement contains two format specifiers. The first one is used to format x as a floating point number to 2 decimal places. The second format specifier is used to format y to 4 decimal places.

3.15 Nested loops

A nested loop is a loop inside a loop. In this example we are using nested **for** loops.

Example 36

```java
// Compute and print out a multiplication table

public class nestedloop
{
    public static void main(String [] args)
    {
        int prod;

        for(int table = 1; table <= 10; table++)
        {
            if (table < 10)
                System.out.print(" ");
            System.out.print(table + " times table ");
            for(int n = 1; n <= 10; n++)
            {
                prod = table * n;
                if (prod < 10)
                    System.out.print(" ");
                if (prod < 100)
                    System.out.print(" ");
                System.out.print(prod + " ");
            }
            System.out.println(" ");
        }
    }
}
```

```
c:\ cmd

E:\JavaDev>java nestedloop
 1 times table   1   2   3   4   5   6   7   8   9  10
 2 times table   2   4   6   8  10  12  14  16  18  20
 3 times table   3   6   9  12  15  18  21  24  27  30
 4 times table   4   8  12  16  20  24  28  32  36  40
 5 times table   5  10  15  20  25  30  35  40  45  50
 6 times table   6  12  18  24  30  36  42  48  54  60
 7 times table   7  14  21  28  35  42  49  56  63  70
 8 times table   8  16  24  32  40  48  56  64  72  80
 9 times table   9  18  27  36  45  54  63  72  81  90
10 times table  10  20  30  40  50  60  70  80  90 100
```

Notes:

1. The control variable n controls the inner loop. It is responsible for printing each number for a given line.

2. The control variable table controls the outer loop. It is responsible for printing each line of the table.

3. The if statements ensure that the times tables are printed in neat columns. They are used to add extra spaces to make sure that the numbers line up.

4. The statement `System.out.println(" ");` makes sure that printing starts on a new line for each new value of table.

Exercise 3-5

1. Write a program which will produce the following output:

```
*
**
***
****
*****
```

2. Write a program that will accept an unknown number of positive integers from the keyboard, terminated by the number −1. The program should determine and display the number of numbers (excluding the data terminator), the smallest and largest numbers.

   (Hint: Let the first number entered at the keyboard be the initial values for minimum and maximum. Then compare the current values for minimum and maximum each time a number is entered.)

Chapter 4 (Week 4)

Sample assignment

4.1 Module 1 Assignment (Specification)

Task 1

The current community charge for a given property in the London borough of Croydon, can be determined from the table below. The total community charge for a year is the sum of the **Croydon services** and **GLA** charge.

Amount of Council tax for the year 2002/2003

Valuation band	Croydon services	GLA
A	453.10	115.92
B	528.62	135.24
C	604.13	154.56
D	679.65	173.88
E	830.68	212.52
F	981.72	251.16
G	1132.75	347.76

You are required to use this information for this part of the assignment.

1. It is suggested that you compile and run each stage of programming, before moving to the next stage.

2. Write a Java program that will allow a user to enter their name, address line 1, address line 2, and post code. The program should give appropriate prompts to help a user enter the data correctly.

3. Extend this program to allow a user to enter a **valuation band** for their property. Include one or more selection statements that will allow the program to determine the amount to be charged for the **Croydon services** and **GLA** for that particular valuation band entered. Use these values to calculate the total chargeable council tax.

4. Extend your program to include a simple validation check to make sure that a valid valuation band has been entered.

5. Extend this program by adding statements that will allow the program to calculate direct debit payments. An initial payment of £120.00 is required followed by 10 equal monthly payments to cover the remainder.

6. Finally, the program should include statements that will output details entered, together with The charge for Croydon services, and GLA, the total community charge, and the initial charge and monthly payments. This information should be displayed in a suitable format.

7. Finally, include appropriate comments to document your program.

8. Explain, giving a range of reasons, the need to test a program. Include a desk check for this program. How do you know that the program always produces correct results?

Task 2

A calculator or for that matter any computer uses a limited amount of storage to store numbers. You may have discovered the problem of overflow while using a calculator. You try to perform a calculation and the result is too large to fit in the allocated space. Instead of obtaining the correct result you usually just get an error message.

If we think of how a real number is represented this should give us an idea to tackle this problem. A real number is made up of two parts a mantissa and exponent.

A real number is then represented as:

$$\mathtt{num\ =\ mantissa\ \times\ 2^{exponent}}$$

This is similar to representing a number in standard form. In standard form we work in base 10. If we were to multiply this number by 10, this can be achieved by adding one to the exponent

Using this idea of standard form, write a program which can compute very large factorials. Use your program to compute 720 factorial.

Include a program listing and screen dump of the working program.

4.2   Solution to task 1 (Program listing)

Example 37

```java
import java.util.Scanner;

public class unit1
{
    public static void main(String args[])
    {
        double croyService = 0.0, gla = 0.0;
        boolean validValBand = true;

        Scanner input = new Scanner(System.in);

        //Enter name and address
        System.out.println("  "); // Blank line
        System.out.print("Enter your name              : ");
        String name = input.nextLine();
        System.out.print("Enter first line of address  : ");
        String address1 = input.nextLine();
        System.out.print("Enter second line of address : ");
        String address2 = input.nextLine();
        System.out.print("Enter postcode               : ");
        String postcode = input.nextLine();

        //Enter validation band
        System.out.print("Enter validation band A - H  : ");
        //Scanner class does not have nextChar()
        String vBand = input.nextLine();
        char valBand = vBand.charAt(0);

        //Select appropriate rate for Croydon services, and GLA
        switch(valBand)
        {

            case 'A':
            case 'a':  croyService = 453.10; gla = 115.92;
                       break;
            case 'B':
            case 'b':  croyService = 528.62; gla = 135.24;
                       break;
            case 'C':
            case 'c':  croyService = 604.13; gla = 154.56;
                       break;
            case 'D':
            case 'd':  croyService = 679.65; gla = 173.88;
                       break;
            case 'E':
            case 'e':  croyService = 830.68; gla = 173.88;
                       break;
            case 'F':
            case 'f':  croyService = 981.72; gla = 251.16;
```

```java
                        break;
            case 'G':
            case 'g':   croyService = 1132.75; gla = 289.90;
                        break;
            case 'H':
            case 'h':   croyService = 1358.30; gla = 347.76;
                        break;

            default:    System.out.println("Invalid valuation" +
                        "band entered"); validValBand = false;
                         break;
        }

    //If valid valuation band - process results
    if (validValBand)
    {
        //Calculations
        double totalCharge = croyService + gla;
        double firstPayment = 120.0;
        double installments =
                          (totalCharge - firstPayment)/10;
        //Round installments to two decimal places
        installments = Math.round(installments* 100);
        installments /= 100;

        //Output results
        System.out.println("  "); // Blank line
        System.out.println("Name                    : " +
                          name);
        System.out.println("Address                 : " +
              address1 + "," + address2 + ", " + postcode);
        System.out.println("Valuation band          : " +
                          valBand);
        System.out.println("Croydon services        : " +
                          croyService);
        System.out.println("GLA                     : " +
                          gla);
        System.out.println("Total community charge : " +
                          totalCharge);
        System.out.println("First payment           : " +
                          firstPayment);
        System.out.println("10 installments of      : " +
                          installments);
    }
}
}
```

4.3 Task 1 (Screen dumps)

Valid valuation band

```
cmd

E:\JavaDev>java unit1

Enter your name              : Tony Hawken
Enter first line of address  : 31 Howden road
Enter second line of address : South Norwood
Enter postcode               : SE25 4AS
Enter validation band A - H  : E

Name                    : Tony Hawken
Address                 : 31 Howden road, South Norwood, SE25 4AS
Valuation band          : E
Croydon services        : 830.68
GLA                     : 173.88
Total community charge  : 1004.56
First payment           : 120.0
10 installments of      : 88.46

E:\JavaDev>
```

Invalid valuation band

```
cmd

E:\JavaDev>java unit1

Enter your name              : Tony Hawken
Enter first line of address  : 31 Howden road
Enter second line of address : South Norwood
Enter postcode               : SE25 4AS
Enter validation band A - H  : J
Invalid valuation band entered

E:\JavaDev>
```

Testing

Testing can be achieved easily by creating a table. In one column enter the results that you obtain using a calculator. In the other column enter the observed result and make sure they match.

There are only 8 possible correct outputs for this program, so you can if you wish test them all.

Notes

The formatting of the amounts of money in this program using round() and integer division is very cumbersome. It would have been much easier to use the printf statement to produce formatted output.

4.4   Solution to Task 2

Example 38

```java
import java.util.Scanner;

public class unit1task2
{
    public static void main(String args[])
    {
        double mantissa = 1.0;
        int exponent = 0;

        Scanner input = new Scanner(System.in);

        System.out.print("Enter factorial required : ");
        int n = input.nextInt();

        for(int c = 1; c < n+1; c++)
        {
            mantissa *= c;
            while (mantissa > 10)
            {
                mantissa /= 10;
                exponent++;
            }
        }

        System.out.print(n + " factorial = ");
        System.out.println(mantissa + " * E+" + exponent);
    }
}
```

```
cmd

E:\JavaDev>java unit1task2
Enter factorial required : 720
720 factorial = 2.6012189435658035 * E+1746
```

Notes:

A printf statement could be used to restrict the number of decimal places.

Chapter 5 (Week 5)

This week will be set aside to complete the assignment. It may also be used to consolidate material. You could start by reading the end of unit summary.

5.1 Tasks to finish

This week is to be used to finish your coursework. At this stage you should have all the skills that you need to complete your coursework. I will include a basic list of tasks that will summarise what you need to do.

By this stage, you should have written a number of programs, compiled and run them. To do this you must have had a familiarity with notepad, so that you can type in a program and save it as Java source code. So, it must have the correct file extension. When you compile and run the program, you need to be familiar with using the command prompt (cmd). A knowledge of a few MS-DOS commands would be useful.

At this stage the programs are likely to be quite simple and short. For that reason, you can probably get away with writing the program without even having to think of a design. I suggest that you build up the program incrementally, only adding a few new features at a time. At each stage, save your work, then compile, and run it. If successful, you can then add bits and continue as before. Working like this means that there is very little scope for errors. If there are any errors, it is likely to be in the few lines that you have just added.

When the programs are completed, you need to make sure that if someone else reads it, they can understand what the program is doing. That is, your programs should be clear and simple (KISS). Also include appropriate comments to explain parts of the program. Another technique used to make your programs more readable is to include blank lines to separate different types of statement, and to use indentation.

The completed program needs to be tested, so that if appropriate data is entered, the program produces the desired results. At this stage we have made very little effort to make sure that a user enters the correct data. You can however add good prompts to indicate to a user the type of data required and also use a validation check to see if the data entered is reasonable.

If the tests suggest that the program is satisfactory, obtain a program listing and a screen dump. The program listing can be inserted into a Microsoft Word document, and so can the screen dump.

5.2 End of Unit Summary

1. A program statement is a complete command. All program statements end with a semicolon.

2. The assignment statement is used to store a result in a given variable.

3. Variables cannot take the name of a reserve word. Nor can they start with a numeric digit, or a punctuation character. Also they cannot contain any punctuation character besides an underscore.

4. You should be familiar with arithmetic operators for integer, float and double operands. Operations such as division behave differently according to whether the operands are of integer type or not.

5. The scope of a variable is the extent of those parts of the program that can access that variable.

6. Variables that can be accessed from anywhere in the program are said to have global scope and are called **global** variables.

7. If a variable is declared within a program block, we say that the scope of the variable is within that block. We call such a variable a **local** variable.

8. Comments. There are 3 types, but only 2 are discussed in this book. C++ comments include the symbol //. Everything after // is ignored by the compiler for the rest of the current line. C-style comments start with /* and end with */. Everything between these two characters is ignored by the compiler.

9. Program indentation is for readability. Programs must be consistently indented to make them more readable.

10. Java is case sensitive. All keywords are always written in lower-case.

11. The names of classes generally start with an uppercase character.

12. There are a number of primitive data types in Java. These include boolean, byte, char, int, float and double.

13. There are also a number of modifiers that effect the size of certain primitive types – in particular an int. These include short and long.

14. The standard binary arithmetic operators are +(add), – (subtract), * (multiply), / (divide), % (remainder).

15. The arithmetic operators follow the normal precedence found in mathematics.

16. The String class is used to create String objects to store character strings. A string is merely a sequence of zero or more characters.

17. The String class contains many methods that can be used to manipulate String objects.

18. The Character class is used to manipulate individual characters.

19. Keyboard input is most easily achieved by creating an object of type Scanner. This object can then call a Scanner method to extract different types of data. For instance, a Scanner object called `kbInput` can extract a number of type double with the statement `kbInput.nextDouble();`

20. The **if** and **switch** statements are used for selection. That is, alternative actions are available depending on whether the expression tested evaluates to true or false.

21. A one-way selection can be performed with an if statement with the following structure:

```
If (expression)
       statement;
```

21. A multi-way selection involves the use of the else clause. The following demonstrates the format of an if-else statement.

```
If (expression1)
        statement1;
else if (expression2)
        statement2;
else
        statement3;
```

22. In Java the switch statement is not very powerful. It can only be used to test variables that are of integer type. Remember that char is also an integer type.

23. A switch statement always contains break statements. When a break is encountered, program execution starts at the end of the switch statement.

24. The for statement is used to repeat code a fixed number of times. It employs a control variable that is used as a counter.

25. A while loop is used when we don't know in advance how many times we want to repeat a certain section of code. The terminating condition appears at the top of the loop and typically tests for a certain value.

26. A data terminator can be used to terminate input, when it is not known in advance how many data items are going to be input.

27. A do... while loop is similar to a while loop, except that the loop-terminating condition comes at the end of the loop.

28. A loop inside a loop is called a nested loop.

Part 2

Further Java programming

Aims

After completing this 5-week unit, you will be able to do the following:

methods

Write a method that can calculate a result and will return the value of this result.

Write a method whose purpose is to perform some action. You could for instance write a method to input values, or display a set of values on the screen

Pass data to methods using parameters.

Arrays

Declare an array, assign values to it and use a loop to process the contents of an array. Be able to solve a variety of problems using arrays

Write functions that can process arrays. Pass an Array as a parameter to a function

Creating classes and objects

Create a class with instance data and instance methods

Create a program with more than one class

Graphics user interfaces

Use the AWT and swing packages to create a simple GUI interface

The GUI should use a container such as JFrame

The GUI should include such components as text fields, text areas, buttons, checkboxes, radio buttons, and pop-down menus.

Use the layout managers – FlowLayout, BorderLayout and GridLayout.

Implement a listener interface so that a user can interact with the GUI components.

Week 6

Arrays and Methods

6.1 Arrays

When processing large amounts of similar data, it makes sense if we can treat this data as a whole. Then we can easily repeat the same operation on the data.

A collection of like data items is called an array. These can be created in Java as follows:

```
int numbers[] = new int [20]; // Array to store 10 integers
char name[] = new char [20];  // Array to store 20 characters
```

All we need to know in advance is how many elements we intend to store in the array.

Individual elements of an array are accessed by reference to an **index**. An index is merely a number that refers to the position within an array. In Java the first element has the index 0. Because we can refer to each element in turn using its index, it is very easy to use a for loop to process the data in an array, making use of the control variable within the for loop to identify the item of data to be processed.

One dimensional arrays or lists can be used to model simple situations where a large stream of data is to be used.

Two dimensional arrays or tables can be used to model such things as multiplication tables, board games such as chess or battleships, the computer screen if we wish to plot some graphics.

Arrays are important in many areas of computing. They can be used to store data that we can then sort, or search for an item of interest.

Unlike C++, an array in Java is like an object and there is an instance variable called length for each array created that stores the size of the array.

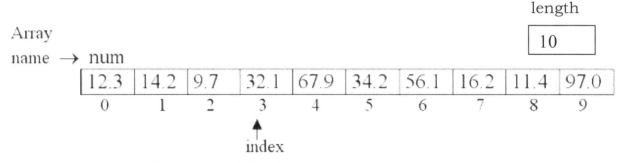

An array of floats

The above array can be declared as follows:

```
float num[] = new float [10];
```

A value can be stored into any chosen position by assignment

```
num[3] = 32.1
```

Questions:

1. What is the 6th element of the above? How could you display it using Java?

2. How can you determine the size of an array?

6.2   Declaring arrays

When you declare an array, you are typically stating what the name of the array is, how many elements it will contain, and the type of each element. This information is necessary to allocate the correct amount of storage.

Example 37

```
public class array1
{
    public static void main(String [] args)
    {
        int dice [] = {1, 2, 3, 4, 5, 6};

        for (int c = 0; c < 6; c++)
            System.out.println("dice[" + c + "] = " + dice[c]);
    }
}
```

```
E:\JavaDev>java array1
dice[0] = 1
dice[1] = 2
dice[2] = 3
dice[3] = 4
dice[4] = 5
dice[5] = 6
```

Notes:

`int dice [];`   is a declaration that creates an array variable dice but allocates no storage. Each element is of type int.

`int dice [6];`   This is forbidden, and would produce a compile error. You cannot specify a size in an array declaration as no storage is allocated.

```
int dice [] = new int [6];
```
This is the correct way to create an array of 6 elements.

```
int dice [] = {1, 2, 3, 4, 5, 6};
```
defines an array with the initial values 1, 2, 3, 4, 5, 6. This method can only be used if you intend to initialize all elements.

6.3   Accessing arrays

Example 38

```java
import java.util.Scanner;

public class array2
{
   public static void main(String [] args)
   {
      double a[] = new double [10];
      double total = 0.0;

      Scanner input = new Scanner(System.in);

      // Store 10 numbers in an array
      for(int c = 0; c < 10; c++)
      {
         System.out.print("Enter next number: ");
         a[c] = input.nextDouble();;
      }

      // Print out contents of array
      for(int c = 0; c < 5; c++)
      {
         System.out.print("a[" + c + "] = " + a[c]);
         System.out.println("\ta[" + (c + 5) + "] = " + a[c + 5]);
      }

      // sum all the elements of an array
      for(int c = 0; c < 10; c++)
          total += a[c];
      System.out.println("\nTotal is " + total);

      // Display smallest element
      double min = a[0];
      for(int c = 1; c < 10; c++)
          if(min > a[c])
              min = a[c];
      System.out.println("\nThe smallest number is " + min);
   }
}
```

Notes:

1. for loops are nearly always used to process arrays. Why?

2. Unlike C or C++ Java can perform boundary checking of the array. This is done using the length

3. The for statements in the previous program, illustrate the way you would process an array if you were writing a C or C++ program. A safer way to process an array is to make use of the length variable. The for statement for the code that sums all the elements of an array could be replaced with this safer version.

```
for(int c = 0; c < a.length; c++)
    total += a[c];
```

Output from array2

```
E:\JavaDev>java array2
Enter next number: 4.6
Enter next number: 3.7
Enter next number: 3.5
Enter next number: 2.7
Enter next number: 5.2
Enter next number: 6.1
Enter next number: 7.2
Enter next number: 8.9
Enter next number: 3.6
Enter next number: 3.9
a[0] = 4.6        a[5] = 6.1
a[1] = 3.7        a[6] = 7.2
a[2] = 3.5        a[7] = 8.9
a[3] = 2.7        a[8] = 3.6
a[4] = 5.2        a[9] = 3.9

Total is 49.4

The smallest number is 2.7
```

6.4   Throwing a die many times

The following program demonstrates some further properties and uses of arrays

Example 39

```java
// Simulation of throwing dice using Math.random(). Can use this
// to demonstrate that the probability of obtaining a given number
// approaches 1/6 as the number of throws increase.

import java.util.Scanner;

public class array3
{
   public static void main(String [] args)
   {
     Scanner input = new Scanner(System.in);

     System.out.print("Enter number of throws : ");
     int numThrows = input.nextInt();

     int numbers[];
     double total1 = 0.0, total2 = 0.0, total3 = 0.0,
              total4 = 0.0, total5 = 0.0, total6 = 0.0;

     // Create array and store numbers thrown
     numbers = new int [numThrows];
     for(int c = 0; c < numbers.length; c++)
         numbers[c] = (int) (6.0 * Math.random() + 1);


     // obtain frequency of each number thrown
     for(int c = 0; c < numbers.length; c++)
         switch(numbers[c])
         {
                 case 1:    total1++; break;
                 case 2:    total2++; break;
                 case 3:    total3++; break;
                 case 4:    total4++; break;
                 case 5:    total5++; break;
                 case 6:    total6++; break;
         }

     // Output numbers 1 - 6
     System.out.println("numbers\t1\t2\t3\t4\t5\t6");

     // output frequencies
     System.out.print("Freq\t" + total1 + "\t" + total2 + "\t");
     System.out.print(total3 + "\t" + total4 + "\t");
     System.out.println(total5 + "\t" + total6);

     // compute length of array
```

```
        int n = numbers.length;

        // output probability of obtaining each number
        System.out.print("average\t" + total1/n + "\t" + total2/n);
        System.out.print("\t" + total3/n + "\t" + total4/n + "\t");
        System.out.println(total5/n + "\t" + total6/n);

    }
}
```

Output:

```
C:\ cmd

E:\JavaDev>java array3
Enter number of throws : 10
numbers 1        2        3        4        5        6
Freq    2.0      2.0      1.0      1.0      1.0      3.0
average 0.2      0.2      0.1      0.1      0.1      0.3

E:\JavaDev>java array3
Enter number of throws : 100
numbers 1        2        3        4        5        6
Freq    17.0     19.0     9.0      20.0     13.0     22.0
average 0.17     0.19     0.09     0.2      0.13     0.22

E:\JavaDev>java array3
Enter number of throws : 1000
numbers 1        2        3        4        5        6
Freq    177.0    164.0    134.0    184.0    184.0    157.0
average 0.177    0.164    0.134    0.184    0.184    0.157

E:\JavaDev>java array3
Enter number of throws : 10000
numbers 1        2        3        4        5        6
Freq    1708.0   1653.0   1645.0   1669.0   1646.0   1679.0
average 0.1708   0.1653   0.1645   0.1669   0.1646   0.1679
```

Notes:

1. `int numbers [];` is used to declare an array variable called numbers (no storage allocated yet).

2. The variables total1 to total6 are used to record the frequencies of obtaining a number 1 to 6.

3. `numbers = new int [numThrows];` creates an array of numThrows integers.

4. `Math.random()` returns a double in the range 0.0 to 1.0.

5. The switch statement is used to increment the appropriate total counter.

6. `numbers.length` returns the length of the array. It is much safer to use this value rather than a specific number that you think points to the last element of the array.

Exercise 6-1

1.   Describe the output generated by the following program:

```
public class demo1
{
    public static void main(String [] args)
    {
        int b = 0;
        int c[10] = { 1, 2, 3, 4, 5, 6, 7, 8, 9, 0 };

        for (int a = 0; a < 10; ++a)
            b += c[a];
        System.out.println("b = " + b);

    }
}
```

2. Write a program that will:

(a)   generate 100 random numbers in the range 1 - 100 and store them in an array.

(b)   calculate and display the minimum, maximum, average of all numbers stored in the array.

3. Write a program that will:

(a)   allow you to enter a number indicating how many Strings you wish to enter at the keyboard

(b)   create an array for storing exactly the number of Strings that you entered.

(c)   print out each String in the array together with the length of the string

(d)   compute and print out the average length of the strings entered.

6.5 Introducing methods

A method is another name for a function in languages such as C or C++. There are two main types of method - instance methods and class methods. This week we will only be considering the latter.

Instance methods require an object to execute them, whereas class methods can be executed without an object. Class methods are declared using the keyword static. We have already come across one such class method - the method `main()`. It has to be declared as static, because it is the first method to run in a program. Before it runs, no objects exist.

You have probably met functions already in the mathematics classroom.

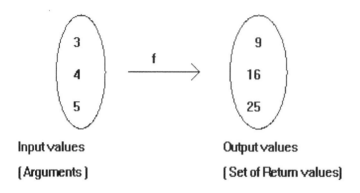

Input values   Output values

[Arguments]   [Set of Return values]

The above function f computes the square number of its input value.

Using standard mathematical notation, we could state:

`f(3) = 9, f(4) = 16, f(5) = 25`

We have already used a number of predefined Java methods in our programs. For instance the `sqrt()` method from the Math class has already been used.

The header of the `sqrt()` method has the following format:

```
static double sqrt(double a)
```

The keyword static tells us that this is a class method. That is we do not need an object to call it. There is a single value of type double which is used to accept the number for which we require the square root. It has a return value of type double which is used to store the square root of the number calculated.

For the following code that involves a method call:

```
double x = 9.0
double y = Math.sqrt(x); //method call
System.out.println(y);
```

We might expect the output: 3.0

6.6   Method to calculate a cube

The following program demonstrates the use of a method.

Example 40

```java
public class method1
{
    public static void main(String [] args)
    {
        for(int c = 1; c <= 5; c++)
            System.out.println(c + "\t" + cube(c));
    }

    static int cube(int n)
    {
        return n * n * n;
    }
}
```

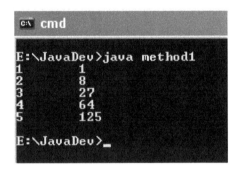

Notes:

1. The keyword static tells us that this is a class method, and so can be executed without an object.

2. All methods generally have a return value. If the return value is of type void, nothing is returned and there is no return statement within the function. In this example an int is returned. The return value is the value of n*n*n.

3. A method is executed when it is called. For instance in the statement System.out.println(c + "\t" + cube(c)); there is the method call cube(c).

4. The parameter c is often referred to as an actual parameter. The value of this parameter is passed to the method cube().

5. The method definition has a parameter called n. This is often referred to as a formal parameter. This parameter accepts the value of c. In effect it behaves like a local variable.

6. The value of n is used by the method to compute a cube, the value of this is returned back to the calling statement.

7. This is the call-by-value parameter passing method.

6.7   Method to determine a minimum

Example 41

```
public class method2
{
    public static void main(String [] args)
    {
        int a = 6, b = 4;
        System.out.println("The minimum value is " + min(a, b));
    }

    static int min(int x, int y)
    {
        if (x < y)
            return x;
        else
            return y;
    }
}
```

```
c:\ cmd

E:\JavaDev>java method2
The minimum value is 4
```

Notes:

1. The method min has two parameters - both integers, and returns an int (the smallest number).

2. The call `min(a, b)` is used to execute the method.

3. Before the method is executed the values of the parameters a and b need to be evaluated. The values of the actual parameters a and b are passed to the formal parameters x and y.

4. These formal parameters are variables local to the method.

5. The variable x is compared with y, if it is the smaller it is returned to the calling statement, otherwise the value of y is.

6. Because the method call is within a println statement, it is the return value that is displayed.

7. Alternatively it is common to see the return value being assigned to another variable.

8. This is another example of calling methods by-value.

6.8   Factorials

The factorial function is much used in mathematics, and is considered to be so important that it appears on all scientific calculators.

The number 5 factorial or 5! is equal to $5 \times 4 \times 3 \times 2 \times 1$.

The following program computes the first 10 factorials.

Example 42

```
public class factorial
{
    public static void main(String [] args)
    {
        for (int n = 1; n <= 10; n++)
            System.out.println("fac(" + n + ") = " + fac(n));
    }

    static long fac(int n)
    {
        int prod = 1;
        for(int c = 1; c <= n; c++)
            prod *= c;
        return prod;
    }
}
```

Notes:

1. prod is a local variable which is only accessible within the method `fac()`.

2. The parameter n is treated as a local variable within `fac()`.

3. The return value is output using the `System.out.println()` statement.

Output:

```
E:\JavaDev>java factorial
fac(1) = 1
fac(2) = 2
fac(3) = 6
fac(4) = 24
fac(5) = 120
fac(6) = 720
fac(7) = 5040
fac(8) = 40320
fac(9) = 362880
fac(10) = 3628800
```

6.9   Method that returns a String

The following program demonstrates that the return value does not have to be a primitive data-type - it can in fact be any type of object.

Example 43

```java
import java.util.Scanner;

public class method3
{
    public static void main(String [] args)
    {
        Scanner input = new Scanner(System.in);

        System.out.print("Enter a number 1-7 :");
        int day = input.nextInt();

        System.out.println("The day entered is " + getDay(day));
    }

    static String getDay(int d)
    {
        String day;
        switch(d)
        {
            case 1:    day = "Monday"; break;
            case 2:    day = "Tuesday"; break;
            case 3:    day = "Wednesday"; break;
            case 4:    day = "Thurdsay"; break;
            case 5:    day = "Friday"; break;
            case 6:    day = "Saturday"; break;
            case 7:    day = "Sunday"; break;
            default:   day = "Invalid data entered"; break;
        }
        return day;
    }
}
```

```
c:\ cmd

E:\JavaDev>java method3
Enter a number 1-7 :3
The day entered is Wednesday
```

Notes:

1. The method `getDay()` has a single parameter of type `int` to accept the day-number.

2. It has a return value of type `String` to return the name of the day.

6.10   A longer example

This example program demonstrates that methods can be called from within other methods. It also demonstrates the use of methods that have no return value - what would in some languages be called procedures.

<u>Example 44</u>

```java
import java.util.Scanner;

public class box
{
   public static void main(String [] args)
   {
     label();
   }

   static void label()
   {
     Scanner input = new Scanner(System.in);

     // Input 3 lines for label
     System.out.print("Enter line 1 : ");
     String line1 = input.nextLine();;
     System.out.print("Enter line 2 : ");
     String line2 = input.nextLine();
     System.out.print("Enter line 3 : ");
     String line3 = input.nextLine();

     //Obtain length for each string
     int l1 = line1.length();
     int l2 = line2.length();
     int l3 = line3.length();

     //Determine maximum string length
     int maxL = max(l1, l2, l3);

     // Output top
     System.out.print("+");
     for(int c = 1; c <= maxL + 2; c++)
         System.out.print("-");
     System.out.println("+");

     // Ouput middle
     printLine(line1, maxL);
     printLine(line2, maxL);
     printLine(line3, maxL);

     // Output bottom
     System.out.print("+");
     for(int c = 1; c <= maxL + 2; c++)
         System.out.print("-");
```

```java
      System.out.print("+");
   }

   static int max(int a, int b, int c)
   {
      return(a > b ? (a > c ? a : c) : (b > c ? b : c));
   }

   static void printLine(String line, int maxLength)
   {
      System.out.print("| " + line);
      int n = maxLength - line.length();
      printSpaces(n + 1);
      System.out.println("|");
   }

   static void printSpaces(int n)
   {
      for(int c = 1; c <= n; c++)
           System.out.print(" ");
   }
}
```

Output:

```
E:\JavaDev>java box
Enter line 1 : A course in programming with QBASIC
Enter line 2 : Tony Hawken
Enter line 3 : Harbin Engineering University press 1995
+-----------------------------------------------+
| A course in programming with QBASIC           |
| Tony Hawken                                    |
| Harbin Engineering University press 1995       |
+-----------------------------------------------+

E:\JavaDev>_
```

Notes:

1. Three strings are input from the keyboard using the method `nextLine()`.

2. The String method `length()` is used to obtain the length of these 3 strings.

3. The method `max()` is used to calculate the maximum length of the 3 strings. The name of each string is passed to the method `max()` for this purpose.

4. The variable maxL is used to store the return value from the method `max()`. That is, it is used to store the maximum length of the 3 strings.

5. The value of maxL is later used in a for loop to control the length of the top and bottom of a box made up of characters used to enclose the strings.

6. The method `printLine()` is used to print 3 lines each of which contains a string and makes up the middle of the box.

7. The method `printLine()` calls the method `printSpaces()`. The method `printSpaces()` is used to print out the necessary number of spaces to the end of the string, so that the the number of characters output on the line is equal to the maximum length of the 3 strings.

Exercise 6-2

1. Write a program that calls a method called `convert()`. This method will convert a temperature in degrees Centigrade to degrees Fahrenheit.

2. Write a method called `leapYear()` which takes one parameter (the year) and will return either true of false depending on whether the year is a leap-year or not.

3. Write a function with the following function header

    ```
    long sumsquares( int n)
    ```

    The function will return the sum of the squares of the integers 1 to n. Write a program that uses this function to print out the sum of the first 20 squares, and the sum of the first 100 squares.

4. Fibonacci numbers can be computed by adding together the two previous numbers. The following is a Fibonacci series:

    1, 1, 2, 3, 5, 8, 13, 21, 34, 55, 89 …….. etc.

    Write a function call fib that has the function header `int fib(int)` that will compute the nth Fibonacci number given the following rules:

    fib(1) = 1, fib(2) = 1, fib(n) = fib(n-2) + fin(n-1)

5. The combination function often referred to as $_nC_r$ in older mathematics textbooks, computes the number of **unordered r element sub-sets** from a set of **n elements**.

    In functional notation this function can be written as :-

    $$C(n, r) = \frac{n!}{r! (n - r)!}$$ Where n! = n factorial = n×(n-1) ×(n-2) ×(n-3) ×…….×3×2×1

    In newer textbooks $_nC_r$ is represented as $\begin{bmatrix} n \\ r \end{bmatrix}$

    (a Write a program that includes a factorial function
    (b) Add to this a combination function that uses the above formula
    (c) Used these functions to compute the binomial coefficients for a given power

An example of a binomial expansion follows:

$$(x+y)^5 = \begin{bmatrix} 5 \\ 0 \end{bmatrix}(x+y)^0 + \begin{bmatrix} 5 \\ 1 \end{bmatrix}(x+y)^1 + \begin{bmatrix} 5 \\ 2 \end{bmatrix}(x+y)^2 + \begin{bmatrix} 5 \\ 3 \end{bmatrix}(x+y)^3 + \begin{bmatrix} 5 \\ 4 \end{bmatrix}(x+y)^4$$
$$+ \begin{bmatrix} 5 \\ 5 \end{bmatrix}(x+y)^5$$

6.11   Using methods to process arrays

In this example we will be using arrays to store statistics, and then using a small collection of static methods to compute the mean, variance and standard deviation. The table below is a grouped frequency table representing marks scored in a small FE college.

Mark	Frequency
1 - 20	8
21 - 30	30
31 - 40	90
41 - 50	103
51 - 60	79
61 - 70	64
71 - 80	21
81 - 90	5

Mean $= \dfrac{\Sigma fx}{\Sigma f} = \mu$ Here Σ denotes sum of

Variance $= \dfrac{\Sigma fx^2}{\Sigma f} - \mu^2 = \sigma^2$

Standard deviation $= \sqrt{\sigma^2} = \sigma$

To use the above statistics we have evaluated a mid-mark **x**. This we can use to calculate estimates for the mean, variance and standard deviation.

Example 45

```java
import java.util.Scanner;

public class stats
{
    public static void main(String [] args)
    {
        double [] x;
        int [] f;

        System.out.print("Enter size of array : ");
        int size = getInteger();

        x = new double [size];
        f = new int [size];

        for(int c = 0; c < size; c++)
        {
            System.out.print("Enter lowest mark in group : ");
            int lowestMark = getInteger();
```

```java
        System.out.print("Enter highest mark in group : ");
        int highestMark = getInteger();
        x[c] = (lowestMark + highestMark) / 2;

        System.out.print("Enter frequency : ");
        f[c] = getInteger();
    }

    displayData(x, f);
    double mean = sumfx(x, f)/ sumf(f);
    double variance = sumfx2(x, f) / sumf(f) - mean * mean;
    double sd = Math.sqrt(variance);

    System.out.println("Mean = " + mean);
    System.out.println("Variance = " + variance);
    System.out.println("Standard deviation = " + sd);
}

static int getInteger()
{
    Scanner input = new Scanner(System.in);

    int mark = input.nextInt();
    return mark;
}

static void displayData(double [] x, int [] f)
{
    System.out.println("x\tf\n");
    for(int c = 0; c < x.length; c++)
        System.out.println(x[c] + "\t" + f[c] );
}

static double sumf(int [] f)
{
    int total = 0;
    for(int c = 0; c < f.length; c++)
        total += f[c];
    return total;
}

static double sumfx(double [] x, int [] f)
{
    double total = 0.0;
    for (int c = 0; c < x.length; c++)
        total += f[c] * x[c];
    return total;
}

static double sumfx2(double [] x, int [] f)
{
    double total = 0.0;
    for (int c = 0; c < x.length; c++)
```

```
            total += f[c] * x[c] * x[c];
        return total;
    }
}
```

Notes:

1. The method `getInteger()` returns the integer entered at the keyboard.

2. x is the mean of **lowestMark** and **highestMark** for each group.

3. The methods **sumf()**, **sumfx()** and **sumfx2()** process one or more arrays. They calculate respectively sum of f, sum of fx and sum of fx^2.

4. An array name is a reference to an array.

5. The parameter passing method is call-by-reference as the parameters are references to an array.

6. With the call-by-reference parameter passing method, the actual objects can be accessed or updated.

Output:

```
c:\ cmd

E:\JavaDev>java stats
Enter size of array : 8
Enter lowest mark in group : 1
Enter highest mark in group : 20
Enter frequency : 8
Enter lowest mark in group : 21
Enter highest mark in group : 30
Enter frequency : 30
Enter lowest mark in group : 31
Enter highest mark in group : 40
Enter frequency : 90
Enter lowest mark in group : 41
Enter highest mark in group : 50
Enter frequency : 103
Enter lowest mark in group : 51
Enter highest mark in group : 60
Enter frequency : 79
Enter lowest mark in group : 61
Enter highest mark in group : 70
Enter frequency : 64
Enter lowest mark in group : 71
Enter highest mark in group : 80
Enter frequency : 21
Enter lowest mark in group : 81
Enter highest mark in group : 90
Enter frequency : 5
x       f

10.0    8
25.0    30
35.0    90
45.0    103
55.0    79
65.0    64
75.0    21
85.0    5
Mean = 47.8
Variance = 220.16000000000003
Standard deviation = 14.837789592793136
```

6.12   Searching and Sorting

In this section we are going to look at some more advanced applications of arrays. This will give you an introduction to the topic of searching and sorting data.

The simplest type of searching technique is called a **Linear Search**. In simple terms this means starting at the beginning of an array and scanning the array one element at a time until the required item is found. The main loop to access the array might look like this :-

```
int i = 0;
while ( i < 10 && num[i] != x)
      i = i ++        // Skip past unwanted items
```

We now need to test which of the two conditions terminated the loop.

```
if (num[i] == x)
      System.out.println("Item found at location " + i);
else
      System.out.println("Item not found");
```

This is an effective method to search for items in an array if the array is very small. But for large arrays it would be very slow as the number of comparisons and hence the time taken is proportional to the number of elements in the array.

A faster method to search for an item in an array is called a Bisection Search. For this to work the items in the array must be sorted.

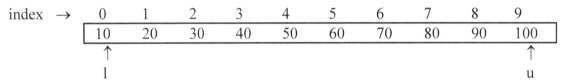

The algorithm goes as follows:

First, guess where the number is by selecting the middle element. The midpoint can be determined by **midpt = (l + u) / 2** . If we perform an integer division it doesn't matter whether we start with an even number or odd number of elements. In this case our initial mid-point will be element 5. We now have 3 possibilities:

1.   number == num[midpt]   // Element is found.

2.   number < num[midpt]   // Search left sublist

3.   number > num[midpt] // Search right sublist

In this case condition 2 applies so we want to search the left sub-list.

To do this set `u = midpt - 1`   **Bisection search after initial comparison**

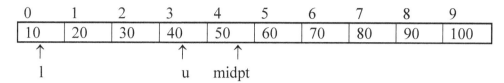

The new mid point can now be calculated with the expression [l + u] / 2 which gives us the value 2. A comparison of `num[midpt]` is made to see whether the element is found etc. This is repeated until either the desired data item is found or u > l.

Sorting is much more complicated than searching and involves many more comparisons. For this reason we will look at the simplest of sorts and leave a more detailed analysis until later. The simplest sort is the **bubble sort**. It contains two components - comparison and interchange. Adjacent elements of an array are compared to see if they are in the correct relative position. If not, they must be swapped round. A strategy for doing that is as follows:

```
if(a[j] < a[j-1])
{
     double temp = a[j];
     a[j] = a[j-1];
     a[j-1] = temp;
}
```

Now a systematic means of ensuring that all elements are compared is required. A bubble sort compares adjacent elements for the entire array, swapping elements that are out of place 1 at a time.

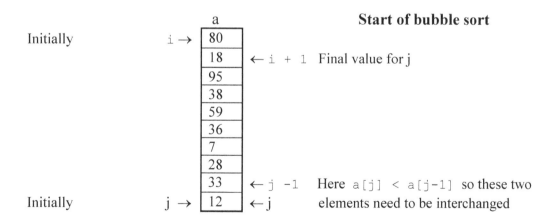

Looking at the previous figure you will see for the first iteration j points to the last element and i to the first. Two elements a[j] and a[j-1] will be compared to see if they are in the correct place. The index j will continually be decremented until it takes a value i+1. Each time adjacent elements will get compared and will be swapped if they are in the wrong order. The complete method for performing a bubble sort should then look like this.

Example 46

```
public class sort
{
    public static void main(String args[])
    {
        int a [] = {80, 18, 95, 38, 59, 36, 7, 28, 33, 12};

        System.out.println("Unsorted data");
        showArray(a);

        sort(a);

        System.out.println("Sorted data");
        showArray(a);

    }

    static void sort(int [] a)
    {
        for(int i = 0; i < a.length; i++)
            for(int j = a.length - 1; j > i; j--)
                if(a[j] < a[j-1])
                {
                    int temp = a[j];
                    a[j] = a[j-1];
                    a[j-1] = temp;
                }
    }

    static void showArray(int [] a)
    {
        for(int c = 0; c < 10; c++)
            System.out.print(a[c] + "   ");
        System.out.println("");
    }
}
```

```
cmd

E:\JavaDev>java sort
Unsorted data
80  18  95  38  59  36  7  28  33  12
Sorted data
7  12  18  28  33  36  38  59  80  95
```

104

6.13   Method overloading

You can use the same name for different methods provided that they have different parameter lists. That is either there are a different number of parameters or the data-types of the parameters are different.

The following are examples of overloaded methods:

```
static int max(int a, int b)
{
    return(a > b ? a : b);
}

static int max(int a, int b, int c)
{
    return(a > b ? (a > c ? a : c) : (b > c ? b : c));
}

static double max( double a, double b)
{
    return(a > b ? a : b);
}
```

Discuss:

Which methods will be used with the following calls:

```
max(2, 5);
```

```
max(4.0, 3.7);
```

```
max(3, 7, 2);
```

Notes:

The C++ language also has this facility and in addition allows you to overload operators. This is forbidden in Java.

6.14   Recursive methods

Recursion is the technique of describing something in terms of itself. So a recursive procedure or function is said to be self-referential. Recursion is an alternative method to iterative algorithms.

The simplest example that appears in many books dealing with the topic of recursion is factorials. One way of describing a factorial is to give an example like the following and then generalise it.

$$5! = 5 \times 4 \times 3 \times 2 \times 1 \qquad (\text{where ! is a short-hand for factorial})$$

More generally we could say:

$$n! = n \times (n\text{-}1) \times (n\text{-}2) \times \ldots \times 3 \times 2 \times 1$$

To be more accurate we would also have to state that $0! = 1$.

We could implement this non-recursively using the following function:

```
static long fac(int n)
{
        int prod = 1;
        for(int c = 1; c <= n; c++)
            prod *= c;
        return prod;
}
```

But if you look at the first definition again you will notice that it can easily be expanded as follows:

$$n! = n \times (n\text{-}1) \times (n\text{-}2) \times \ldots \times 3 \times 2 \times 1$$

$$\Rightarrow \quad n! \quad = \quad n \times (n\text{-}1)!$$
$$(n\text{-}1)! = (n\text{-}1) \times (n\text{-}2)!$$
$$(n\text{-}2)! = (n\text{-}2) \times (n\text{-}3)!$$
$$.$$
$$.$$
$$.$$
$$3! \quad = 3 \times 2!$$
$$2! \quad = 2 \times 1!$$
$$1! \quad = 1 \times 0! \qquad \text{and we know what } 0! \text{ is. } 0! = 1 \text{ by definition.}$$

These expressions are called recurrence relations. If we take the most general expression which is:

$$n! = n \times (n\text{-}1)!$$

and the terminating condition $0! = 1$, we can easily write a recursive function to do the same thing.

Now is the time to explain how recursion works.

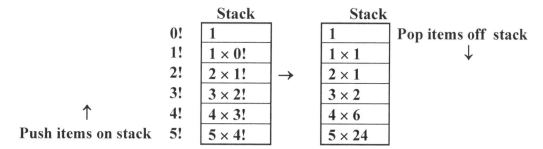

Recursive evaluation of 5!

Each time a recursive call is made, it is stored on the stack ready to be used at a later time. When a termination condition arises (0! = 1) this stops. The first item is popped off the stack and the value substituted into the expression below. This continues until the last item on the stack is removed. By this time 5! has been evaluated.

Example 47

```java
public class factorial2
{
    public static void main(String args[])
    {
        for (int n = 1; n <= 10; n++)
            System.out.println("fac(" + n + ") = " + fac(n));

    }

    static int fac(int n)
    {
        if (n == 1)
            return 1;
        else
            return(n * fac(n-1));
    }

}
```

```
c:\ cmd

E:\JavaDev>java factorial2
fac(1) = 1
fac(2) = 2
fac(3) = 6
fac(4) = 24
fac(5) = 120
fac(6) = 720
fac(7) = 5040
fac(8) = 40320
fac(9) = 362880
fac(10) = 3628800
```

6.15   Two dimensional arrays

A two dimensional array is sometimes called a table. A two dimensional array has two subscripts instead of one. It is a very common structure in everyday life. Objects like chess boards, the screen of your monitor made up of pixels and maps all have a tabular structure and hence can be represented using two-dimensional arrays. The simplest is possibly the multiplication table.

×	1	2	3	4	5	6	7	8	9	10
1	1	2	3	4	5	6	7	8	9	10
2	2	4	6	8	10	12	14	16	18	20
3	3	6	9	12	15	18	21	24	27	30
4	4	8	12	16	20	24	28	32	36	40
5	5	10	15	20	25	30	35	40	45	50
6	6	12	18	24	30	36	42	48	54	60
7	7	14	21	28	35	42	49	56	63	70
8	8	16	24	32	40	48	56	64	72	80
9	9	18	27	36	45	54	63	72	81	90
10	10	20	30	40	50	60	70	80	90	100

col → (top), row → 1 (left)

The following code demonstrates the use of 2-dimensional arrays:

Example 48

```
public class timestables
{
    public static void main(String args[])
    {
        int [][] table = new int [10][10];
        int row, col;

        //Store values in table
        for(row = 0; row < 10; row++)
            for(col = 0; col < 10; col++)
                table[row][col] = (row + 1) * (col + 1);

        // Print the table
        for(row = 0; row < 10; row++)
        {
            for(col = 0; col < 10; col++)
                System.out.print(table[row][col] + "\t");
            System.out.println("");
        }
    }
}
```

```
E:\JavaDev>java timestables
1       2       3       4       5       6       7       8       9       10
2       4       6       8       10      12      14      16      18      20
3       6       9       12      15      18      21      24      27      30
4       8       12      16      20      24      28      32      36      40
5       10      15      20      25      30      35      40      45      50
6       12      18      24      30      36      42      48      54      60
7       14      21      28      35      42      49      56      63      70
8       16      24      32      40      48      56      64      72      80
9       18      27      36      45      54      63      72      81      90
10      20      30      40      50      60      70      80      90      100

E:\JavaDev>_
```

Notes:

1. The 2D array table containing integers is declared using:

```
int [][] table = new int [10][10];
```

2. A nested for loop is used to access the 2D array. The inner for loop selects the column position, starting at 0, and progresses to col = 9. Once this happens, the row value is incremented. Then each of the column positions is revisited for the new row position.

3. Within the first loop, it is necessary to multiply together (row + 1) and (col + 1) to obtain each value in the table. This is because the first element in an array has an index of 0.

4. In the second loop, a tab is used within the inner loop to space the numbers. At the end of the row, a `println()` statement is used to go to the next line.

Exercise 6-3

1. Describe the output produced when the following program is run.

```
public class Mystery
{
    public static void main(String [] args)
    {
        int start = 3, c;

        int [] arr = new int [10];

        for(c = 0; c < arr.length; c++)
            arr[c] = start += 2;

        for(c = 1; c < arr.length - 1; c++)
            arr[c] = arr[c-1] + arr[c+1];

        for(c = 0; c < arr.length; c++)
            System.out.print(arr[c] + "\t");
    }
}
```

2. Write a program which will:

(a) Create an array called list capable of holding 20 numbers.

(b) Populate this array using random numbers in the range 1 to 50.

(c) Sort the array called list with a bubble sort.

(d) Search for one of the numbers using a bisection search.

3. Write a program that will include methods to compute both the minimum and maximum of up to 4 numbers. You should consider including methods for each primitive data-type that you may want to use. Test these methods with a set of calls in your main method.

4. Fibonacci numbers can be defined by the recurrence relations:

$$F_1 = 1 , \ F_2 = 1 \ , \ F_n = F_{n-1} + F_{n-2}$$

(a) Write a program that has a statement that will create an empty array called fibNum that can be used to store 100 Fibonacci numbers.
(b) Store the value 1 in the first two elements of the array.
(c) Write a method called getFib() that will compute the next Fibonacci number based on the two previous Fibonacci numbers.
(d) Write a method called displayArray() that will display the contents of fibNum.

Week 7

Classes and objects

7.1 Introduction to classes and objects

Writing programs that require the use of classes and objects is referred to as **object-oriented programming**. Every Java program has at least one class, so in a sense all Java programs are **object-oriented**. Up until now we really have not used the classes defined in our programs, in that we have not used the classes we have defined to create objects. It could be said that we have been using the procedural paradigm whilst programming with an object-oriented language.

A class is composed of **member data** and **member functions**. The member functions are usually called **methods**. When you create an object, you are creating an instance of the class. The object created contains an instance of all the member data defined in the class, together with a reference to all methods defined in the class.

You can think of a class as being a new data type as you can create objects using a class, in much the same way that you define variables to create storage for the primitive data types.

7.2 Creating classes and objects

In this section we will extend our ideas about classes by introducing both instance variables and instance methods. You will now notice that we have to create objects, so that we can use these instance methods. We have now included variables within our class. Instance variables which are associated with a particular object, and class variables which are associated with a class as a whole. The following program illustrates all of these points.

Example 49

```java
import java.util.Scanner;

public class Circle
{
    // class variables
    static int count = 0;

    // instance variables
    double radius;
    double x, y;
```

```java
    //instance methods

    double circumference()
    {
      return 2 * Math.PI* radius;
    }

    double area()
    {
      return Math.PI * radius * radius;
    }

    void getCircleData()
    {
      Scanner input = new Scanner(System.in);
      System.out.print("Enter radius : ");
      radius = input.nextDouble();
      System.out.print("Enter x : ");
      x = input.nextDouble();
      System.out.print("Enter y : ");
      y = input.nextDouble();
    }

    // Driving method
    public static void main(String [] args)
    {
      // create a Circle object
      Circle c1 = new Circle();

      // Store data in Circle object
      c1.getCircleData();

      // Display Circumference of circle
      System.out.println("Circumference = " + c1.circumference());

      // Display area of circle
      System.out.println("Area = " + c1.area());
    }
}
```

```
cmd

E:\JavaDev>java Circle
Enter radius : 3.5
Enter x : 4.7
Enter y : 5.2
Circumference = 21.991148575128552
Area = 38.4845100064749
```

Notes:

1. All class variables are identified as such using the keyword static

2. A class variable belongs to the class as a whole, not to a particular instance or object.

3. All other variables declared within a class are instance variables.

4. Instance variables are contained within each object created.

5. Instance variables are accessed using instance methods.

6. A class method is identified by the keyword static. All other methods are instance methods.

7. Each instance method has a variable called this. The variable this is used to store the name of the object that is calling the method.

8. There are two types of instance method – accessor and mutator methods. Accessor methods are those that make no changes in the instance data of an object. Typically they are used to display values or use the values of an object to perform a calculation. Mutator methods are those that update the data within an object. Typically if you don't initialize an object, you need to add the data later. You will need mutator methods to do this.

9. The statement `Circle c1 = new Circle();` creates an object of type Circle by calling the constructor `Circle()`.

10. Each class has a default constructor created by the compiler. This is used each time a new object is created.

11. A programmer can define their own constructors, which override the default constructor.

12. The statement `c1.getCircleData()` is used to store data in the variables of the object c1. We say that the object c1 has called the method `getCircleData()`.

7.3   Constructors

A constructor is a special type of method to create objects. A constructor is a method that has the same name as the class. A constructor is used for creating new objects.

 This process of creating an object is called instantiation. That is, creating an instance of the class. They are also responsible for initializing instance variables for the object being created.

The following can be added to the previous program:

Example 50

```
// constructors

Circle2()
{
  count++;
  radius = 0.0;
  x = 0.0;
  y = 0.0;
}

Circle2(double r)
{
  count++;
  radius = r;
  x = 0.0;
  y = 0.0;
}

Circle2(double r, double xC, double yC)
{
  count++;
  radius = r;
  x = xC;
  y = yC;
}
```

Notes:

1. A constructor is a method with the same name as the class.

2. A constructor does not have a return value.

3. A constructor is executed every time an object is created.

4. If you write your own constructors they override those created by the compiler.

5. Constructors can be overloaded.

6. Constructors are invoked using the new operator.

The following modified `main()` method can be used to demonstrate how constructors are used. This method replaces the one in the previous program.

Example 51

```java
// Driving method

public static void main(String [] args)
{
    // create Circle2 objects
    Circle2 c1 = new Circle2();
    Circle2 c2 = new Circle2(5);
    Circle2 c3 = new Circle2(4, 2, 3);

    // output instance variables for each object
    System.out.println("\tradius\tx\ty");
    System.out.println("c1\t" + c1.radius + "\t" + c1.x + "\t" + c1.y);
    System.out.println("c2\t" + c2.radius + "\t" + c2.x + "\t" + c2.y);
    System.out.println("c3\t" + c3.radius + "\t" + c3.x + "\t" + c3.y);

    // Compute circumference and area
    System.out.println("\tCircumference\tArea");
    System.out.println("c1\t" + c1.circumference() + "\t" + c1.area());
    System.out.println("c2\t" + c2.circumference() + "\t" + c2.area());
    System.out.println("c3\t" + c3.circumference() + "\t" + c3.area());

    // Output the number of objects created
    System.out.println("The program has created " + count +" objects");
}
}
```

```
cmd

E:\JavaDev>java Circle2
        radius   x       y
c1      0.0      0.0     0.0
c2      5.0      0.0     0.0
c3      4.0      2.0     3.0
        Circumference    Area
c1      0.0      0.0
c2      31.41592653589793        78.53981633974483
c3      25.132741228718345       50.26548245743669
The program has created 3 objects
```

Notes:

1. Three Circle2 objects are created using 3 different overloaded constructors.

2. Which constructor is invoked, is determined by the number of parameters entered.

3. Instance variables in this example can be accessed without using any of the methods of the class. This is not good programming practice, and should be avoided, as we will see in a later section.

4. The count variable is a class variable, and in this example is being used to count how many objects have been created.

115

Exercise 7-1

1. What is the difference between a class and an object?

2. What is the difference between an instance variable and a class variable?

3. What is the difference between an instance method and a class method?

4. Explain what a constructor is, and what it is used for.

5. Create a class called Rectangle which:
   a. contains two fields called length and width
   b. contains methods to compute perimeter and area of the rectangle
   c. contains a method to display the current state of an object
   d. contains constructors for creating Rectangle objects
   e. contains a main method to create objects and test the other methods

6. Type in and complete the following code for the constructors and methods for the fraction class below replacing the comments – put code here, with the necessary code to carry out the required actions.

```java
import java.util.Scanner;

public class Fraction
{
   //Instance variables
   int n;
   int d;

   //constructors
   Fraction()      //Default constructor
   {}

   Fraction(int num, int den)
   {
        //(1) Code goes here
   }

   //accessor methods

   void displayData()
   {
        //(2) Code goes here
   }

   //mutator methods

   void enterData()
   {
        //(3) Code goes here
   }
```

```java
    //arithmetic methods
    Fraction addFraction(Fraction a)
    {
        Fraction c = new Fraction();
        c.n = n * a.d + d * a.n;
        c.d = d * a.d;

        return c;
    }

    Fraction subFraction(Fraction a)
    {
        // (4) Code goes here
    }

    Fraction mulFraction(Fraction a)
    {
        // (5) Code goes here
    }

    Fraction divFraction(Fraction a)
    {
        // (6) Code goes here
    }

    //Driver method
    public static void main(String [] args)
    {
        Fraction x = new Fraction();
        x.enterData();
        x.displayData();

        Fraction y = new Fraction(3, 4);
        y.displayData();

        Fraction z = new Fraction();
        z = x.addFraction(y);
        z.displayData();
    }
}
```

The output generated should look like this

```
E:\JavaDev>java Fraction
Enter numerator : 2
Enter denomintor : 5
2/5
3/4
23/20

E:\JavaDev>_
```

7.4 Including more than one class in your programs

The following program illustrates the fact that you can have more than one class in each program file. In this case one class is used for producing objects and the other is used to contain the main method that is used to run the program.

Example 52

```java
//import java.util.Scanner;

class Circle3
{

   // class variables
   static int count = 0;

   // instance variables
   double radius;
   double x, y;

   //instance methods

   double circumference()
   {
     return 2 * Math.PI* radius;
   }

   double area()
   {
     return Math.PI * radius * radius;
   }


   // constructors

   Circle3()
   {
     count++;
     radius = 0.0;
     x = 0.0;
     y = 0.0;
   }

   Circle3(double r)
   {
     count++;
     radius = r;
     x = 0.0;
     y = 0.0;
   }

   Circle3(double r, double xC, double yC)
   {
```

```
            count++;
            radius = r;
            x = xC;
            y = yC;
        }
}

public class testCircle
{
    public static void main(String [] args)
    {
    // create Circle3 objects
    Circle3 c1 = new Circle3();
    Circle3 c2 = new Circle3(5);
    Circle3 c3 = new Circle3(4, 2, 3);

    // output instance variables for each object
    System.out.println("\tradius\tx\ty");
    System.out.println("c1\t" + c1.radius + "\t" + c1.x + "\t" +
    c1.y);
    System.out.println("c2\t" + c2.radius + "\t" + c2.x + "\t" +
    c2.y);
    System.out.println("c3\t" + c3.radius + "\t" + c3.x + "\t" +
    c3.y);

    // Compute circumference and area
    System.out.println("\tCircumference\tArea");
    System.out.println("c1\t" + c1.circumference() + "\t" +
    c1.area());
    System.out.println("c2\t" + c2.circumference() + "\t" +
    c2.area());
    System.out.println("c3\t" + c3.circumference() + "\t" +
    c3.area());

    // Output the number of objects created
        System.out.println("The program has created " +
        Circle3.count + " objects");
    }
}
```

Notes:

1. This program is essentially the same as Circle2, and produces exactly the same output

2. There are two classes in the program - Circle3 and testCircle

3. Only one of the classes is allowed to be declared as public - this is always the one with the method main in it.

4. The program was saved as `testCircle.java` - and so will be compiled with the command: `javac testCircle.java`

5. Compiling this program will produce two **.class** files containing bytecode.

6. To run the program type `java testCircle`. This will execute the byte-code in `testCircle.class` and also incorporate the byte-code in `Circle3.class`.

7. To access the count variable within main we have to refer to it as Circle3.count, to let the compiler know what class it is to be found in.

You can obtain a brief summary of the fields and methods contained within a .class file by using the `javap` command.

```
cmd
E:\JavaDev>javap testCircle
Compiled from "testCircle.java"
public class testCircle extends java.lang.Object{
    public testCircle();
    public static void main(java.lang.String[]);
}
```

Likewise the contents of the Circle3 class file can also be displayed and will look like this:

```
cmd
E:\JavaDev>javap Circle3
Compiled from "testCircle.java"
class Circle3 extends java.lang.Object{
    static int count;
    double radius;
    double x;
    double y;
    double circumference();
    double area();
    Circle3();
    Circle3(double);
    Circle3(double, double, double);
    static {};
}
```

When you run testCircle the following output is obtained.

```
cmd
E:\JavaDev>java testCircle
        radius    x        y
c1      0.0       0.0      0.0
c2      5.0       0.0      0.0
c3      4.0       2.0      3.0
        Circumference    Area
c1      0.0       0.0
c2      31.41592653589793        78.53981633974483
c3      25.132741228718345       50.26548245743669
The program has created 3 objects
```

120

7.5   Access modifiers

Parts of a Java program can be protected from others parts of the program by specifying the types of access different objects can have. The **public** keyword indicates that that part of the program is accessible from any part of the program - it is in fact **global**. The most restrictive form of access is **private**. To summarize the following tables follow:

Class

Modifier	Meaning
public	This is accessible from all classes
abstract	Cannot create objects from this class. Can only use this to create other classes.
final	No subclasses can be declared from this

Field

Modifier	Meaning
public	Can be accessed from within all classes
protected	Can be accessed from within its own class and all its sub-classes
private	Can only be accessed from within its own class (use class method)
static	Only one value exists for each class, not for each object
transient	Not part of the persistent state of an object
volatile	Compiler cannot modify for optimisation purposes
final	Must be initialised and cannot be changed

Method

Modifier	Meaning
public	Can be accessed from within all classes
protected	Can be accessed from its own class and its subclasses
private	Can only be accessed from within its own class
abstract	Method has no body and belongs to an abstract class
final	No subclasses can override it
static	Is a class method and so doesn't need an object to call it
native	body of method is implemented in another language
synchronised	Must be locked before a thread can invoke it

Constructor

Modifier	Meaning
public	This is accessible from all other classes
protected	This is accessible from within its own class and all subclasses
private	This is accessible from within its own class only

The previous tables are included for completeness only. I will not attempt to illustrate many of these modifies. On the next page there follows a program that illustrates the use of some of the more commonly used modifiers.

121

7.6   Using a drinks machine

The following program is a longer example that demonstrates the use of: classes, instance data, instance methods, constructors and Access modifiers.

<u>Example 53</u>

```java
import java.util.Scanner;

class DrinksMachine
{
   // The drinks dispenser is initially half-filled with
   // fifty of each coin
   private static int onePenny = 50;
   private static int twoPenny = 50;
   private static int fivePenny = 50;
   private static int tenPenny = 50;
   private static int twentyPenny = 50;
   private static int fiftyPenny = 50;
   private static int onePound = 50;
   private static int twoPound = 50;

   // The dispenser will stop dispensing when any of the
   // coinage containers are full or empty
   private int empty = 0;
   private int full = 100;

   DrinksMachine() {}

   // Display levels of individual coins
   int onePenny() { return onePenny; }
   int twoPenny() { return twoPenny; }
   int fivePenny() { return fivePenny; }
   int tenPenny() { return tenPenny; }
   int twentyPenny() { return twentyPenny; }
   int fiftyPenny() { return fiftyPenny; }
   int onePound() { return onePound; }
   int twoPound() { return twoPound; }

   // Add coins
   void addOnePenny(int onePenny){ this.onePenny += onePenny;}

   void addTwoPenny(int twoPenny){ this.twoPenny += twoPenny;}

   void addFivePenny(int fivePenny){ this.fivePenny += fivePenny;}

   void addTenPenny(int tenPenny){ this.tenPenny += tenPenny;}

   void addTwentyPenny(int twentyPenny)
   { this.twentyPenny += twentyPenny;}

   void addFiftyPenny(int fiftyPenny){ this.fiftyPenny += fiftyPenny;}

   void addOnePound(int onePound){ this.onePound += onePound;}

   void addTwoPound(int twoPound){ this.twoPound += twoPound;}
```

```java
// Remove coins for change

void removeOnePenny(int onePenny){this.onePenny -= onePenny;}

void removeTwoPenny(int twoPenny){ this.twoPenny -= twoPenny;}

void removeFivePenny(int fivePenny){ this.fivePenny -= fivePenny;}

void removeTenPenny(int tenPenny){ this.tenPenny -= tenPenny;}

void removeTwentyPenny(int twentyPenny)
{ this.twentyPenny -= twentyPenny;}

void removeFiftyPenny(int fiftyPenny){ this.fiftyPenny -= fiftyPenny;}

void removeOnePound(int onePound){ this.onePound -= onePound;}

void removeTwoPound(int twoPound){ this.twoPound -= twoPound;}

int insertCoins()
{
   Scanner input = new Scanner(System.in);

   int amount = 0;  // calculate amount in pence
   System.out.print("Enter number of two pound coins : ");
   int a = input.nextInt();
   amount += 200 * a;
   addTwoPound(a);
   System.out.print("Enter number of one pound coins : ");
   int b = input.nextInt();
   amount += 100 * b;
   addOnePound(b);
   System.out.print("Enter number of fifty pence coins : ");
   int c = input.nextInt();
   amount += 50 * c;
   addFiftyPenny(c);
   System.out.print("Enter number of twenty pence coins : ");
   int d = input.nextInt();
   amount += 20 * d;
   addTwentyPenny(d);
   System.out.print("Enter number of ten pence coins : ");
   int e = input.nextInt();
   amount += 10 * e;
   addTenPenny(e);
   System.out.print("Enter number of five pence coins : ");
   int f = input.nextInt();
   amount += 5 * f;
   addFivePenny(f);
   System.out.print("Enter number of two pence coins : ");
   int g = input.nextInt();
   amount += 2 * g;
   addTwoPenny(g);
   System.out.print("Enter number of one pence coins : ");
   int h = input.nextInt();
   amount += h;
   return amount;   // amount entered
}
```

```java
int menu()
{
   Scanner input = new Scanner(System.in);

   System.out.print("1.  Large Coca Cola \t 55p\t");
   System.out.println("6.  Large Tea      \t 47p");
   System.out.print("2.  Medium Coca Cola\t 42p\t");
   System.out.println("7.  Medium Tea     \t 33p");
   System.out.print("3.  Small Coca Cola \t 30p\t");
   System.out.println("8.  Large Coffee  \t 65p");
   System.out.print("4.  Large Milk      \t 37p\t");
   System.out.println("9.  Medium Coffee \t 65p");
   System.out.print("5.  Small Milk      \t 22p\t");
   System.out.println("10. Hot Chocolate \t 40p\n");
   System.out.print("Enter your choice : ");
   int choice = input.nextInt();

   switch(choice)
   {
        case 1: return 55;
        case 2: return 42;
        case 3: return 30;
        case 4: return 37;
        case 5: return 22;
        case 6: return 47;
        case 7: return 33;
        case 8: return 65;
        case 9: return 65;
        case 10: return 40;
        default: System.out.println("Invalid choice entered");
                 return 0;
   }
}

void calculateChange(int changeRequired)
{
   int coin200, coin100, coin50, coin20, coin10, coin5, coin2, coin1;
   coin200=coin100 = coin50 = coin20 = coin10 = coin5 = coin2 =
    coin1 =0;

   while(changeRequired > 0)
   {
        if (changeRequired >= 200)
        {
             coin200++;
             removeTwoPound(1);
             changeRequired -= 200;
        }
        else if (changeRequired >= 100)
        {
             coin100++;
             removeOnePound(1);
             changeRequired -= 100;
        }
        else if (changeRequired >= 50)
        {
             coin50++;
             removeFiftyPenny(1);
```

```
                    changeRequired -= 50;
            }
            else if (changeRequired >= 20)
            {
                    coin20++;
                    removeTwentyPenny(1);
                    changeRequired -= 20;
            }
            else if (changeRequired >= 10)
            {
                    coin10++;
                    removeTenPenny(1);
                    changeRequired -= 10;
            }
            else if (changeRequired >= 5)
            {
                    coin5++;
                    removeFivePenny(1);
                    changeRequired -= 5;
            }
            else if (changeRequired >= 2)
            {
                    coin2++;
                    removeTwoPenny(1);
                    changeRequired -=2;
            }
            else if (changeRequired >= 1)
            {
                    coin1++;
                    removeOnePenny(1);
                    changeRequired--;
            }
        }
    }
    System.out.println("Your change will contain the following" +
                       "coins :");
    if (coin200 > 0)
        System.out.println("two pound coins   \t" + coin200);
    if (coin100 > 0)
        System.out.println("one pound coins   \t" + coin100);
    if (coin50 > 0)
        System.out.println("fifty pence coins \t" + coin50);
    if (coin20 > 0)
        System.out.println("twenty pence coins\t" + coin20);
    if (coin10 > 0)
        System.out.println("ten pence coins   \t" + coin10);
    if (coin5 > 0)
        System.out.println("five pence coins  \t" + coin5);
    if (coin2 > 0)
        System.out.println("two pence coins   \t" + coin2);
    if (coin1 > 0)
        System.out.println("one pence coins   \t" + coin1);
    }
}


public class GetDrinks
{
    public static void main(String [] args)
    {
```

```
        DrinksMachine x = new DrinksMachine();
        int cost = x.menu();
        int amountEntered = x.insertCoins();
        int changeRequired = amountEntered - cost;
        x.calculateChange(changeRequired);
    }
}
```

```
c:\ cmd

E:\JavaDev>java GetDrinks
1.   Large Coca Cola      55p    6.   Large Tea          47p
2.   Medium Coca Cola     42p    7.   Medium Tea         33p
3.   Small Coca Cola      30p    8.   Large Coffee       65p
4.   Large Milk           37p    9.   Medium Coffee      65p
5.   Small Milk           22p   10.   Hot Chocolate      40p

Enter your choice : 2
Enter number of two pound coins : 0
Enter number of one pound coins : 0
Enter number of fifty pence coins : 0
Enter number of twenty pence coins : 3
Enter number of ten pence coins : 0
Enter number of five pence coins : 0
Enter number of two pence coins : 0
Enter number of one pence coins : 0
Your change will contain the following coins :
ten pence coins         1
five pence coins        1
two pence coins         1
one pence coins         1

E:\JavaDev>_
```

Notes:

1. The drinks-dispenser is initially allocated with 50 of each coin.

2. A variable for each coin-type is used to maintain a coin-count.

3. If the coin-count reaches 100 it is considered full and no more coins of this type can be accepted. If coin count goes down to 0, it is considered empty. Consequently this coin-type cannot be used to give change.

4. An object of type DrinksMachine called x is created using the constructor DrinksMachine().

5. This is used to call the menu() method. This method allows a user to choose what drink they want to buy from a menu. It returns the price of the drink chosen.

6. The method insetCoins() allows a user to specify how many of each type of coin they intend to enter. It returns the total value of coins entered.

7. The change required is determine by subtracting the cost from the value of coins entered.

8. The method `calculateChange()` takes a single parameter – the change required, and will determine the coins to issue for change, starting with the largest coin value that can be used to give the correct change.

9. This same method will display the number of each coin given out for change.

7.7   Using dialog boxes for input and output

Dialog boxes are provided by the JoptionPane class. A dialog box looks exactly like a pop-up Window. It has similar properties to the windows that you are familiar with. We will be looking at two types – one to display text or messages, the other to accept user input.

The following program is based on a previous program. All I have done is changed the method for input and output.

Example 54

```
// Convert Centigrade to Fahrenheit

import javax.swing.*;

public class temp3
{
    public static void main(String [] args)
    {
        String temp;   //String to input temperature

        temp = JOptionPane.showInputDialog("Enter temperature"
             + " (degrees C) : ");

        float c = Float.parseFloat(temp);

        float f = 9/5 * c + 32;

        JOptionPane.showMessageDialog(null, "The temperature "
                + c + " degrees Centigrade \n is " + f
                + " degrees Fahrenheit", "Results",
                JOptionPane.PLAIN_MESSAGE);
    }
}
```

When you run the program, you obtain the following dialog box to input data.

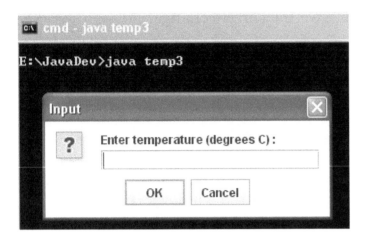

If I were to type in 25 and click on OK, I obtain the following.

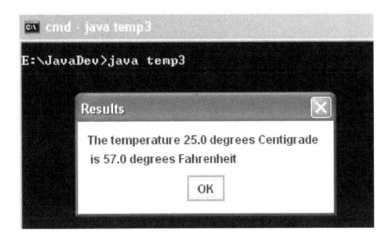

If I click on OK in this dialog box, the window will close.

Notes:

1. The `showInputDialog()` method is used for user input. It has a parameter which is used to specify a user prompt.

2. It has a return value of type String. This is used to store the user input.

3. You will notice that the input dialog box has two buttons. If the user input has been typed in correctly, you are expected to click on OK. If you have made a mistake you can clear the input and start again by clicking on cancel.

4. This user input needs to be converted to the required data type. In this case float. The method `parseFloat()` is used for this purpose.

5. The method `showMessageDialog()` is used to display output on the screen.

6. This method has four parameters. The first – null, indicates that the message will appear at the centre of the screen. The second is the message, that is the output you wish to display. The third is used for the title on the bar of the message window. Finally, the last parameter indicates the type of message – in this case a plain message.

Exercise 7-2

1. Making use of the data that follows create a class called planet. Create another class called TestPlanets that will create planet objects.

(a) Your planet class should include constructors, access methods and methods to insert data.

(b) Your TestPlanets class should create at least two planet objects and illustrate some of the planet methods.

(c) Create a method to calculate the gravitational field strength of a given planet. Use the formula:

$$g = GM/r^2 \quad where\, G = 6.67 \times 10^{11}$$
$$M = \text{mass of planet in Kg}$$
$$r = \text{radius of planet in m}$$

Note: Numbers can be entered in exponential format.

e.g. double G = 6.67E11;

Name	Mass$\times 10^{24}$ Kg	radius $\times 10^3$ m	distance from sun $\times 10^9$m	T = 1 revolution (Earth years)
Mercury	0.328	2437	57.9	0.24
Venus	4.871	6050	108.25	0.62
Earth	5.977	6367	149.6	1
Mars	0.642	3387	227.9	1.88
Jupiter	1901	714400	778.3	11.96
Saturn	569.01	60000	1427	29.46
Uranus	87.00	26150	2870.3	84.01
Neptune	103.0	24300	4496.6	164.79
Pluto	0.0118	1210	5900	247.7

2. Redo program example 18 (solving a quadratic equation) using 3 input dialog boxes and an output dialog box in place of using the scanner class and a `println()` statement.

Chapter 8 (Week 8)

Creating Graphics user interfaces

8.1 Graphical User Interfaces

Many application programs today use a graphical User Interface (GUI). That is, facilities for using a program are more graphical in nature, and that a user will be using a mouse probably more than the keyboard. A GUI is characterized by components such as buttons, lists, checkboxes and radio buttons that require a user to click on with a mouse to interact with the program.

Whilst this is usually easier for a user to use, it is much more difficult for a programmer to write. However, Java makes this easier than for many other languages, as there are many classes and associated methods that allow a programmer to write programs with a graphical user interface.

8.2 The AWT package

The java.awt package or Abstract Windows Toolkit is the earliest available facility within Java that allowed the writing of programs with graphical user interfaces. It contains many packages, and in all contains hundreds of classes. The classes can be roughly divided into 3 main categories:

1.   Graphics - colours, fonts, images, lines and polygons

2.   Components - GUI components such as frames, buttons, menus, lists etc.

3.   Layout Managers - these classes control the layout of components

The Graphics class contains many methods for drawing using points, and lines etc. It also has methods for drawing various shapes such as rectangles, polygons, circles and ovals. The Graphics class will be left until next week. Here we will be creating Graphics objects inside applets.

We will use mainly the **Component class** in this section to create simple graphical user interfaces. The Component class is an abstract class, and is a super-class of many other classes.

The component class contains for example – buttons, text boxes, text areas, lists, check boxes and radio buttons. Most people will be familiar with all of these, as they frequently appear on the Internet.

A **container** is a component that can contain other components. Frames and windows are examples of containers as they can contain components such as buttons and text-boxes. Containers can also contain other containers. The

130

Container class is an abstract class and a super-class of other classes that define containers.

A Window is a container with additional properties, such as a tool-kit for creating components.

A frame is a window that has a title bar, a menu bar, a border and a cursor etc. Frames are the main type of window used for drawing graphics and creating GUIs.

8.3 The swing package

The AWT components were the first to be used for writing GUI applications within Java. How an AWT component appears depends on the environment in which the program is being run – mac OSX, Windows, Linux, or X-Windows etc. In each case the AWT components take on the appearance of the operating system that the program is being run on.

The swing package is a newer development in Java. It also provides GUI components, and these components are based on the AWT. Unlike the AWT components, swing components provide a consistent appearance no matter what operating system is being used. It is for this reason that Swing components are much more commonly used than the AWT equivalents.

You can tell whether a component comes from the swing class, as they all start with a capital J. So for example, the Button class from within the AWT is called JButton if we use the equivalent swing component. The components to be found in the swing package are very closely related to the components to be found in the AWT. In fact the swing classes directly inherit properties from the AWT classes.

Even if we are going to use the swing package for all of our components, we will still in addition have to use the AWT package in all of our GUI programs. The graphics class is only obtainable from the AWT. Also, we will need to use the AWT packages to be able to interact with the components. This is because all of the event managers are within the AWT packages and nowhere else.

8.4 Creating simple Windows using the JFrame class

The JFrame class is used for creating JFrame objects which look and behave like Windows. A JFrame is an example of a component - that is something which can be displayed on the screen and interact with a user. The interaction is provided by clicking on the available buttons. JFrame inherits properties from the Frame class in the AWT libraries.

Example 55

```java
import javax.swing.*;

class testFrame
{
    public static void main(String [] args)
    {
      JFrame frame = new JFrame("Example frame");
      frame.setSize(250,100);
      frame.setVisible(true);
    }
}
```

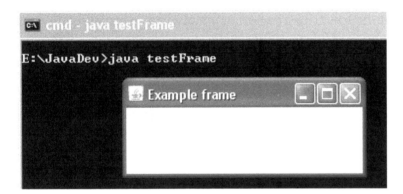

Notes:

1. `JFrame frame1 = JFrame("Example frame);` invokes a JFrame constructor which creates a JFrame object called frame1 and inserts "Example frame" in the JFrame title.

2. The `setSize()` method is used to set the size of the frame. In this case 250 × 100 pixels.

3. The `setVisible()` method is used to make the frame visible. For the frame to be visible, the method has to have the parameter `true`. If you want to hide the frame, the parameter `false` is used.

4. To maximize the frame, click on the middle button.

5. To minimize the frame, click on the left button.

6. To terminate the program click on the right button.

8.5 The Color class

Objects of the Color class are used to specify colours in graphics operations and as we will soon see are used to change the background colours of frames and other related objects.

The colour of an object can be identified by a three-component RGB code. The standard colours defined in the Color class are as follows:

object	RGB code
Color.black	(0,0,0)
Color.blue	(0,0,255)
Color.cyan	(0,255,255)
Color.darkGray	(64,64,64)
Color.gray	(128,128,128)
Color.green	(0,255,0)
Color.lightGray	(192,192,192)
Color.magenta	(255,0,255)
Color.orange	(255,200,0)
Color.pink	(255,175,175)
Color.red	(255,0,0)
Color.white	(255,255,255)
Color.yellow	(255,255,0)

This can be illustrated as follows:

Example 56

```
import java.awt.*;

class Frame2
{
    public static void main(String [] args)
    {
        Frame frame = new Frame("");
        frame.setBackground(Color.green);
        frame.setSize(200,120);
        frame.setTitle("Frame with a colour background");
        frame.setVisible(true);
    }
}
```

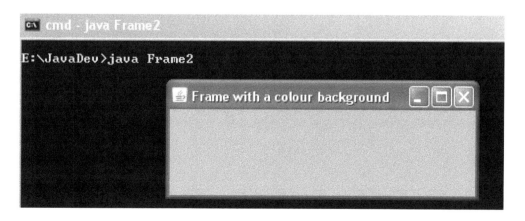

Notes:

1. The **Frame** class in the AWT package is very similar to the JFrame class in the swing package.

2. The **Color** class is defined in the **AWT** package.

3. The **Frame()** constructor used has no parameters, so no title is included when the Frame object frame is created.

4. The **setBackground()** method is used to set the background colour to green.

5. It is possible to choose from 16,777,216 different colours.

6. You can create your own colours as follows:

   ```
   Color myColour = new Color(25, 90, 155);
   ```

7. The **setTitle()** method is used to add a title to a frame.

8.6 Using a constructor for your class

The example below is based on example 55. Here we have created a constructor for the class TestJFrame2.

Example 57

```
import javax.swing.*;

class testJFrame2 extends JFrame
{
   public testJFrame2()
   {
     JFrame frame1 = new JFrame("Example frame");
     setSize(250,100);
     setVisible(true);
   }

   public static void main(String [] args)
   {
     testJFrame2 frame = new testJFrame2();
   }
}
```

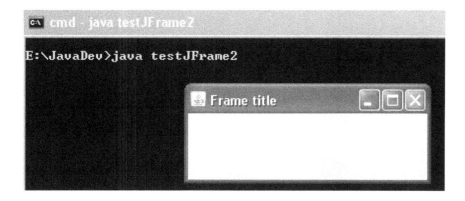

Notes:

1. The clause extends JFrame is used to specify that the class testJFrame2 inherits properties from the class JFrame.

2. In this example we have included a constructor that specifies the properties that we want to give to a TestJFrame2 object. This is a much more flexible approach as it enables us to create a number of JFrame objects easily with the same basic properties.

8.7   Creating Labels

A label is a means of storing text within a Frame or Window. A user cannot interact with a Label, it is merely used for storing information. You can use a label to store a heading, display a paragraph of text, or to display results of a calculation.

Example 58

```java
import javax.swing.*;
import java.awt.*;

class Label
{
   public static void main(String [] args)
   {
     JFrame frame = new JFrame("Label in a frame");
     frame.setSize(250, 100);
     JLabel label = new JLabel("Labels can be used as headings");
     frame.add(label);
     frame.setVisible(true);
   }
}
```

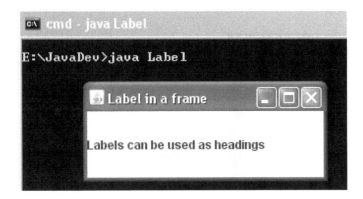

The following example achieves the same result as for Example 58. This time a constructor is used to create the frame with a label.

Example 59

```java
import javax.swing.*;
import java.awt.*;

class Label2 extends JFrame
{
   public Label2(String s)
   {
     super(s);
     setSize(250, 100);
     JLabel label = new JLabel("Labels can be used as headings");
     add(label);
     setVisible(true);
   }


   public static void main(String [] args)
   {
     Label2 label = new Label2("Label in a Frame");
   }
}
```

Notes:

1. A new JLabel object called label, is created by calling the constructor `JLabel()`. In this example `JLabel()` has a parameter – a string. This string stores the text that will appear in the label.

2. The JLabel object called label is added to the frame using the `add()` method.

8.8 Using text fields and text areas

A text field is a component that allows a user to enter up to a single line of text. You typically specify the maximum number of characters that can be entered. A text area is used to enter several lines of text.

Example 60

```
import javax.swing.*;
import java.awt.*;
import java.awt.event.ActionEvent;
import java.awt.event.ActionListener;

class Text extends JFrame
{
   JLabel promptName;
   JTextField firstName, initial, lastName;
   JTextArea address;

   Text(String s)
   {
     super(s);                // invoke constructor of parent class
     setSize(400,300);
     setLayout(new FlowLayout());

     promptName = new JLabel("Enter your name in this order: First
                             name, initial, Last name ");
     add(promptName);
     firstName = new JTextField(10);
     add(firstName);
     initial = new JTextField(1);
     add(initial);
     lastName = new JTextField(10);
     add(lastName);
     address = new JTextArea("Enter your address here ", 4, 30);
     add(address);

     setVisible(true);
   }

   public static void main(String args [])
   {
     Text t1 = new Text("Enter name and address");
   }
}
```

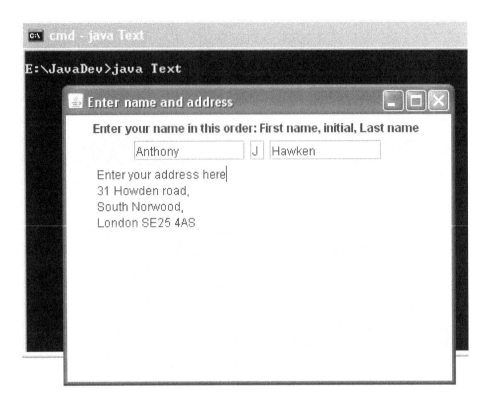

Notes:

1. The `JTextField()` constructor is always used to create a new object of type JTextField.

2. The `JTextField()` constructor is overloaded. It can have zero parameters. In this case you just get an empty text field.

3. It can take a string that contains text that will initially be stored in the text field.

4. The `JTextArea()` contstructor is also overloaded. It can have no parameters. It can have a string containing text that will appear in the text area.

5. Normally when you create a `JTextArea()` object you include 2 numbers – the number of rows and columns. In addition, you can also include a string containing text that is to be initially stored in the text area.

8.9 Creating buttons

A button is a component that has a label and can respond when the user clicks on it with a mouse.

Demonstration of the Button class

Example 61

```java
import javax.swing.*;
import java.awt.*;

class Frame3
{
   public static void main(String [] args)
   {
      JFrame frame = new JFrame("frame with a button");
      frame.setBackground(Color.red);
      frame.setSize(250, 100);
      frame.setLocation(400,50);
      JButton button = new JButton("Click me");
      frame.add(button);
      frame.setVisible(true);
   }
}
```

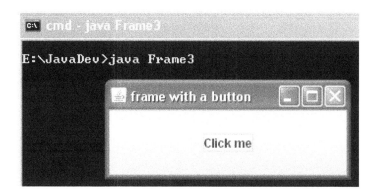

Notes:

1. The statement frame.setLocation(400,50); sets the initial location of the frame on the screen

2. The object button is an instance of Button, and has a label "Click me".

3. The method setLabel() can be used to change the label on a button.

4. The statement frame.add(button); is used to add the object button to the JFrame object called frame.

8.10   Creating Layouts

The arrangement of several components within a frame is called a layout. We will look at the following layouts:

Flowlayout is used to place the components in order, so as to fill up the available space.

GridLayout specifies how the components are to be placed according the the parameters passed to the GridLayout constructor.

BorderLayout uses the concept of borders - North, South, East, West and Center.

If you are going to add more than one component, you will always have to include a layout. If you don't, the second and subsequent components will overwrite the first.

Demonstration of FlowLayout

Example 62

```
import javax.swing.*;
import java.awt.*;

class ButtonFrame extends JFrame
{
   ButtonFrame(String s)
   {
     super(s); // runs the Frame(String s) constructor
     setSize(300,200);
     setLayout(new FlowLayout());
     for(int i=0; i<6; i++)
         add(new JButton("button" + i));
     setVisible(true);
   }

   public static void main(String [] args)
   {
     ButtonFrame buttonFrame = new ButtonFrame("FlowLayout demo");
   }
}
```

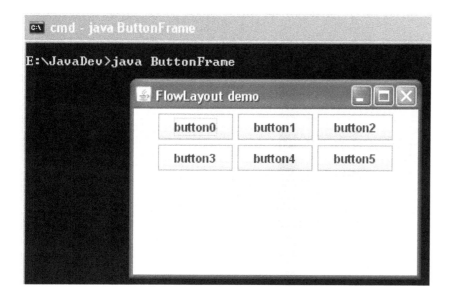

Note:

The buttons are placed in order across the screen - to fill the available space in the frame. Any other buttons are now placed on the next line.

Demonstrate GridLayout

The **GridLayout** class enables you to specify the format of the layout in terms of the number of rows and columns. The following program demonstrates this.

Example 63

```java
import javax.swing.*;
import java.awt.*;

class ButtonFrame2 extends JFrame
{
   ButtonFrame2(String s)
   {
     super(s);
     setSize(300,200);
     setLayout(new GridLayout(4,3));
     for (int i=1; i<=12; i++)
             add(new JButton("Button " + i));
     setVisible(true);
   }

   public static void main(String[] args)
   {
     new ButtonFrame2("Demonstrate GridLayout");
   }
}
```

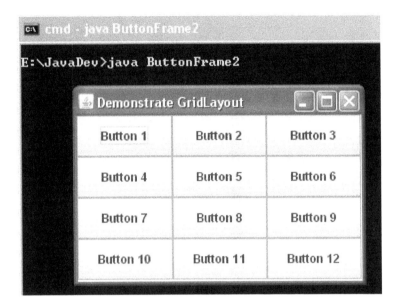

Notes:

The constructor call **GridLayout(4,3)** specifies that the controls are to be organised in 4 rows and 3 columns.

Demonstration of BorderLayout

Example 64

```java
import javax.swing.*;
import java.awt.*;

class ButtonFrameBorder extends JFrame
{
    ButtonFrameBorder(String s)
    {
        super(s);
        setSize(250,250);

        JButton north = new JButton("North");
        JButton south = new JButton("South");
        JButton west = new JButton("West");
        JButton east = new JButton("East");
        JButton centre = new JButton("Centre");

        setLayout(new BorderLayout());
        add(north , BorderLayout.NORTH);
        add(south , BorderLayout.SOUTH);
        add(west , BorderLayout.WEST);
        add(east , BorderLayout.EAST);
        add(centre , BorderLayout.CENTER);
        setVisible(true);
    }
```

```
  public static void main(String [] args)
  {
    new ButtonFrameBorder("ButtonFrameBorder example");
  }
}
```

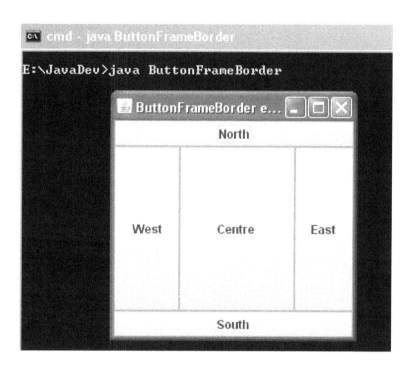

Notes:

The position of components when you use BorderLayout is determined by the
keywords: NORTH, SOUTH, WEST, EAST, and CENTER.

Exercise 8-1

1. Write a Java program that creates a frame with 4 buttons. The buttons should
   have the following text on them - "Rewind", "Play", "Fast Forward" and "Stop".
   Experiment with different layouts.

2. Refer back to a previous program used to solve quadratic equations. Design a
   clear but simple graphical user interface to provide user input for the
   quadratic coefficients a, b, and c. Also consider how the results will be
   displayed. You are to use labels and text boxes. You will not be able to retrieve
   the data input to do the calculations at this stage (this comes later). This is
   purely an exercise in designing a simple interface.

8.11   Other components

In this section we will be looking at some other GUI components. The first is a JCheckBox. This is the Swing version of CheckBox. The second example uses the AWT component Choice that is used to implement a drop-down menu. Later on in the book we will see a Swing component that does a similar job – JComboBox.

Checkboxes

Example 65

```java
import javax.swing.*;
import java.awt.*;

class CheckboxFrame extends JFrame
{
    JCheckBox cb1, cb2, cb3, cb4, cb5, cb6, cb7, cb8;

    CheckboxFrame(String s)
    {
      super(s);
      setSize(400, 200);
      setLayout(new GridLayout(4,2));

      cb1 = new JCheckBox("Mathematics");
      cb2 = new JCheckBox("Further Mathematics");
      cb3 = new JCheckBox("Physics");
      cb4 = new JCheckBox("Chemistry");
      cb5 = new JCheckBox("Biology");
      cb6 = new JCheckBox("English");
      cb7 = new JCheckBox("History");
      cb8 = new JCheckBox("Geography");

      //add checkboxes
      add(cb1); add(cb2); add(cb3); add(cb4);
      add(cb5); add(cb6); add(cb7); add(cb8);

      setVisible(true);
    }

    public static void main(String args [])
    {
      CheckboxFrame cbf = new CheckboxFrame("CheckBox demo");
    }
}
```

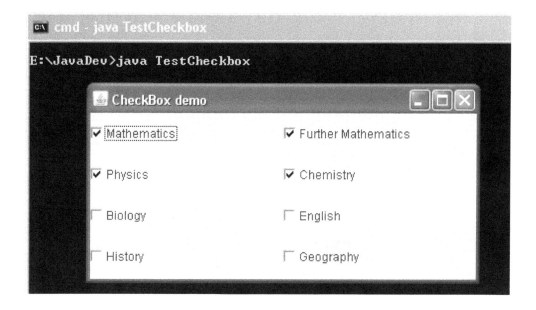

Notes:

A checkbox is used to indicate yes or no. If you click on such a checkbox, a tick will appear. Click again, and the tick is removed. In the above run of the program, I have clicked on the top 4 checkboxes.

A simple drop-down menu

The Choice component is from the AWT package. It is used to implement a drop-down menu. To select an item from the drop-down menu, you just click on it.

Example 66

```java
import javax.swing.*;
import java.awt.*;

class ChoiceFrame extends JFrame
{
    ChoiceFrame(String s)
    {
        super(s);
        setSize(400, 200);
        Choice c = new Choice();
        c.add("Mathematics");
        c.add("Further Mathematics");
        c.add("Physics");
        c.add("Chemistry");
        c.add("Biology");
        c.add("English");
        c.add("History");
        c.add("Geography");
        add(c);
        setVisible(true);
    }
}
```

```
class testChoice
{
   public static void main(String args [])
   {
     ChoiceFrame cf = new ChoiceFrame("Choice demo");
   }
}
```

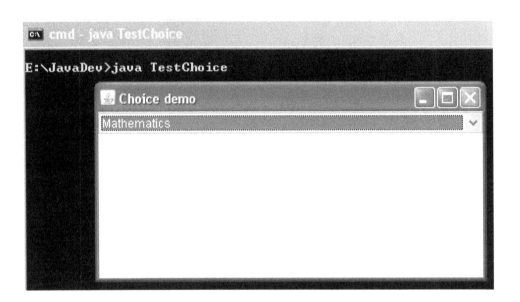

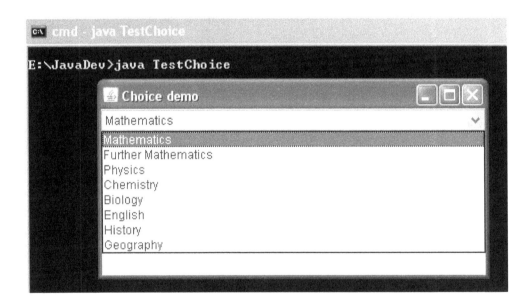

Notes:

1. `c.add("Mathematics");` adds the "Mathematics" option to the Choice object c.

2. `add(c);` adds the object c to the frame

8.12   Event-driven programming

To make components of a GUI such as buttons work you have to implement the "listener interface" so that the container (JFrame) is able to "hear" them.

An event-driven program is simply a program that runs an event loop which waits for user-input and then responds appropriately when such input is detected. User-input in the context of event-driven programs typically takes the form of clicking and dragging a mouse rather than using a keyboard.

8.13   The button-click event

Example 67

```
import javax.swing.*;
import java.awt.*;
import java.awt.event.ActionEvent;
import java.awt.event.ActionListener;

class ButtonFrame extends JFrame implements ActionListener  // (1)
{
    JButton button;

    ButtonFrame(String s)
    {
      super(s);                 // invoke constructor of parent class
      setSize(200,100);
      setLayout(new FlowLayout());
      button = new JButton("Click me!");                    // (2)
      add(button);
      button.addActionListener(this);
      setVisible(true);
    }

    public void actionPerformed(ActionEvent event)          // (3)
    {
      if (event.getSource() == button)
          System.out.println("Button clicked!");
    }
}

class TestButtonFrame
{
    public static void main(String args [])
    {
      ButtonFrame buttonframe = new ButtonFrame("demo click");
    }
}
```

This is obtained when you run the program for the first time.

Once you click the button, you obtain this.

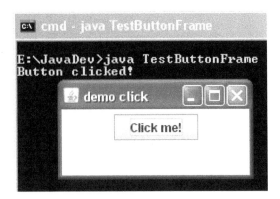

Notes:

1. To make **buttonFrame** objects responsive to events such as a button-click we need to make it an **action listener**.

2. This is done by (1) adding the implements **ActionListener** clause to the declaration of the class, (2) registering each of the buttons with a call to the **addActionListener()** method and (3) implementing the **actionPerformed()** interface.

3. Because the **ButtonFrame** object buttonframe is an **actionListener**, then it will create an **ActionEvent** object whenever an event occurs. At this point the method **ActionPerformed()** will be invoked, and the **ActionEvent** object will be passed as a parameter.

4. The **actionPerformed() interface** is a template for a method that you must implement. Within the **actionPerformed()** method you can test what type of event has occurred. You then specify what action you want performed for any given event that has just occurred.

5. In this example there is a test to see whether the button has been clicked. We test this by testing the source of the event - the object called button.

6. The action to be performed if this is the case, is to display "Button clicked!".

8.14 Inserting text into a JTextField

This example demonstrates how you can retrieve text entered in a text field.

Example 68

```java
import javax.swing.*;
import java.awt.*;
import java.awt.event.ActionEvent;
import java.awt.event.ActionListener;

class Temp extends JFrame implements ActionListener        // (1)
{
   JTextField text;
   JLabel prompt, answer;

   Temp(String s)
   {
     super(s);              // invoke constructor of parent class
     setSize(300,150);
     setLayout(new FlowLayout());
     prompt = new JLabel("Enter a temperature - degrees c");
     add(prompt);
     text = new JTextField(3);
     add(text);
     text.addActionListener(this);                          // (2)
     answer = new JLabel();
     add(answer);
     setVisible(true);
   }

   public void actionPerformed(ActionEvent event)           // (3)
   {
     if (event.getSource() == text)
     {
         String cTemp = text.getText();
         double c = Double.parseDouble(cTemp);
         double f = 9.0 * c /5.0 + 32.0;
         answer.setText("The temperature in degrees F is " + f);
     }
   }

   public static void main(String args [])
   {
     Temp t1 = new Temp("Temperature conversion");
   }
}
```

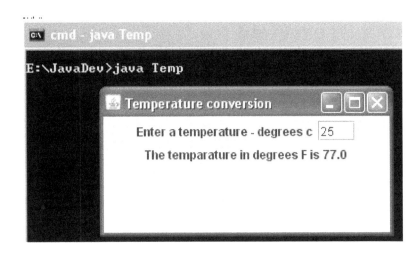

Notes:

1. All components need to be added to the JFrame container. The `add()` method is used to add each of the components to the JFrame container.

2. To make the text fields in the class Temp responsive to events it is necessary to make them an **action listener**.

3. This is achieved by (1) adding the **implements ActionListener** clause to the declaration of the class Temp, and (2) registering the text field as an action listener. Finally, the interface **actionPerformed()** must be implemented (3). Implementing the interface **actionPerformed()** means filling in the contents of the method to state what you want performed by this method should an event occur.

4. The object prompt is a **label**. A label is a container for storing text, but cannot be edited. In this case it is being used to prompt the user to enter a temperature in degrees C.

5. The object **text** is a **text field** big enough to enter and display 3 characters. This is used to enter the temperature in degrees c. Adding text in this text field will activate the `method actionPerformed()`.

6. Firstly, when activated the method `actionPerformed()` obtains a string containing the temperature in degrees c using the method `getText()`. From this a double will be extracted and stored in c. The value of c is used to calculate the temperature in degrees F.

7. The object answer is also a label. It is used to output the answer in degrees F. The last thing that **actionPerformed()** does is to set the value of this label to the computed temperature in degrees F. The `setText()` method is used to add the results to the label answer. The text comprising these results will now appear on the screen.

8.15   Other types of Event

To reiterate, when you write a program with a graphical user interface (GUI), certain types of interaction with components within the GUI involves an event-driven model. So for example when a user enters text into a text field or clicks on a button, the program must respond to these actions by creating an **event** that can be detected by an **event handler**. The event handler is a method that can detect these events, and execute appropriate code when such events are detected.

The Java programmer writes such an event handler called a **listener**. This listener will constantly check whether an event has occurred and respond accordingly. The listener is created by implementing a **listener interface**. This is merely a blank template for a method that will correspond to certain types of event.

In the previous example, we implemented the **ActionListener** interface. This particular interface works with Text fields, text areas and buttons. When you write an event handler for this, it must use the interface `actionPerformed()`, and this always has a single parameter of type **ActionEvent**. The class that contains the event handler must implement the ActionListener Interface, and all of the components must be registered as a listener.

Different types of GUI component work with different types of listener interface. These are summarized in the table below.

JComponent	User action required	Event object created	Listener interface
JTextField JTextArea JButton	Enter data and press return. For a button – click it.	ActionEvent	ActionListener
JRadioButton JCheckBox JComboBox	Select an item (Can deselect a checkbox also)	ItemEvent	ItemListener
JList	Select an item	ListSelectionEvent	ListSelectionListener
Any component	Press or release mouse button Move or drag the mouse	MouseEvent	MouseListener MouseMotionListener

8.16 Using Checkboxes

The following example uses check boxes to allow a user to select the subjects they wish to study.

Example 69

```java
import javax.swing.*;
import java.awt.*;
import java.awt.event.*;

public class CBFrame extends JFrame
{
    private JCheckBox cb1, cb2, cb3, cb4, cb5, cb6, cb7, cb8;
    private Container contents;

    public CBFrame(String s)
    {
        super(s);
        contents = getContentPane();

        setSize(400, 200);
        contents.setLayout(new GridLayout(4,2));

        //Create checkboxes
        cb1 = new JCheckBox("Mathematics");
        cb2 = new JCheckBox("Further Mathematics");
        cb3 = new JCheckBox("Physics");
        cb4 = new JCheckBox("Chemistry");
        cb5 = new JCheckBox("Biology");
        cb6 = new JCheckBox("English");
        cb7 = new JCheckBox("History");
        cb8 = new JCheckBox("Geography");

        //add checkboxes to Frame
        contents.add(cb1); contents.add(cb2);
        contents.add(cb3); contents.add(cb4);
        contents.add(cb5); contents.add(cb6);
        contents.add(cb7); contents.add(cb8);

        //Create TestCheckBox event handler object
        TestCheckBox tcb = new TestCheckBox();
        //Register event handler with checkboxes
        cb1.addItemListener(tcb); cb2.addItemListener(tcb);
        cb3.addItemListener(tcb); cb4.addItemListener(tcb);
        cb5.addItemListener(tcb); cb6.addItemListener(tcb);
        cb7.addItemListener(tcb); cb8.addItemListener(tcb);

        setVisible(true);
    }

private class TestCheckBox implements ItemListener
```

```
{
  public void itemStateChanged(ItemEvent ie)
  {
    //Check each checkbox for a change of state
    if (ie.getSource() == cb1)
        if (ie.getStateChange() == ItemEvent.SELECTED)
            System.out.println("Mathematics");

    if (ie.getSource() == cb2)
        if (ie.getStateChange() == ItemEvent.SELECTED)
            System.out.println("Further Mathematics");

    if (ie.getSource() == cb3)
        if (ie.getStateChange() == ItemEvent.SELECTED)
            System.out.println("Physics");

    if (ie.getSource() == cb4)
        if (ie.getStateChange() == ItemEvent.SELECTED)
            System.out.println("Chemistry");

    if (ie.getSource() == cb5)
        if (ie.getStateChange() == ItemEvent.SELECTED)
        System.out.println("Biology");

    if (ie.getSource() == cb6)
        if (ie.getStateChange() == ItemEvent.SELECTED)
            System.out.println("English");

    if (ie.getSource() == cb7)
        if (ie.getStateChange() == ItemEvent.SELECTED)
            System.out.println("History");

    if (ie.getSource() == cb8)
        if (ie.getStateChange() == ItemEvent.SELECTED)
            System.out.println("Geography");
  }
}

  public static void main(String args [])
  {
    CBFrame cbf = new CBFrame("CheckBox demo");
  }
}
```

Notes:

1. Check boxes cb1 to cb8 are created using the `JCheckBox()` constructor. A parameter is used with this constructor so that each check box is labled.

2. All of the check boxes added need to be added to the frame. The `add()` method is used for this purpose.

3. All of the check boxes need to be registered as an `addItemListener` object. Firstly, an event handler called TestCheckBox is created. Then each of the check boxes is registered with the event handler object.

4. There is a private class called TestCheckBox that is used to manage the event handling. Within it, there is a method called `itemStateChanged()`. This is an implementation of the `itemStateChanged()` inteface.

5. An interface is merely an empty template of a method that must be used. All we have had to do is supply the contents to state what is to happen when certain events occur.

6. In particular, the method `getSource()` is used to determine which check box has been clicked. If a check box has been clicked, the check box is marked as selected. In this program this state value is determine. If selected, a message is displayed for that check box.

7. Many if statements are used instead of a single if ... else statement, because it is possible for several check boxes to be checked at the same time.

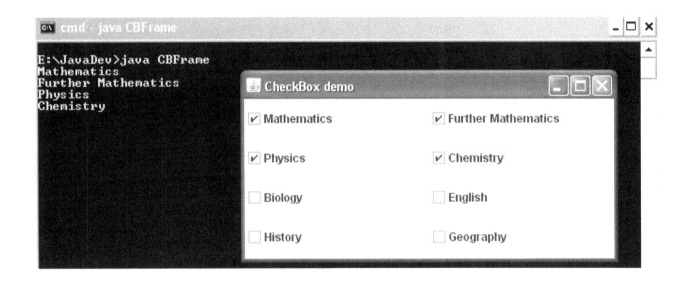

8.17   Using Radio buttons

The following example uses radio buttons to enter an age group. You will notice that it is very like the previous example that uses checkboxes.

Example 70

```
import javax.swing.*;
import java.awt.*;
import java.awt.event.*;

public class Radio extends JFrame
{
    private JRadioButton age1, age2, age3, age4, age5, age6;
    private ButtonGroup age;
    private Container contents;

    public Radio(String s)
    {
      super(s);
      contents = getContentPane();

      setSize(400, 200);
      contents.setLayout(new FlowLayout());

      //Create radio buttons
      age1 = new JRadioButton("Under 16");
      age2 = new JRadioButton("17-25");
      age3 = new JRadioButton("26-35");
      age4 = new JRadioButton("36-45");
      age5 = new JRadioButton("46-55");
      age6 = new JRadioButton("56-65");

      //add radio buttons to Frame
      contents.add(age1); contents.add(age2);
      contents.add(age3); contents.add(age4);
      contents.add(age5); contents.add(age6);

      //Create Radio button group
      age = new ButtonGroup();
      age.add(age1); age.add(age2);
      age.add(age3); age.add(age4);
      age.add(age5); age.add(age6);

      //Create TestRadioButton event handler object
      TestRadioButton trb = new TestRadioButton();
      //Register event handler with radio buttons
      age1.addItemListener(trb); age2.addItemListener(trb);
      age3.addItemListener(trb); age4.addItemListener(trb);
      age5.addItemListener(trb); age6.addItemListener(trb);

      setVisible(true);
```

155

```
    }

private class TestRadioButton implements ItemListener
{
    public void itemStateChanged(ItemEvent ie)
    {
      //Check each checkbox for a change of state
      if (ie.getSource() == age1)
          System.out.println("age: Under 16");
      else if (ie.getSource() == age2)
          System.out.println("age: 17 - 25");
      else if (ie.getSource() == age3)
          System.out.println("age: 26 - 35");
      else if (ie.getSource() == age4)
          System.out.println("age: 36 - 45");
      else if (ie.getSource() == age5)
          System.out.println("age: 46 - 55");
      else if (ie.getSource() == age6)
          System.out.println("age: 56 - 65");
    }
}

    public static void main(String args [])
    {
      Radio rb = new Radio("Radio button demo");
    }
}
```

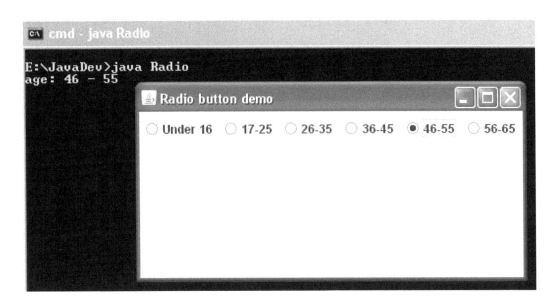

Notes:

1. 6 radio buttons age1 to age6 are created using a JButton constructor.

2. All of the radio buttons are added to the container object called contents. Using a container object is an alternative to using a JFrame object. They are being used for the same purpose

156

3. A ButtonGroup called age is created so that all of the radio buttons can be associated with it. That is, they act as a group of radio buttons, only one of which can be selected at any one time.

4. Each of the radio buttons is registered as an **item listener** using the addItemListener() method and is associated with an event handler object called trb.

5. There is a private class called TestRadioButton that implements ItemListener.

6. Within this, the interface **itemStateChanged()** has been implemented. Implementing the itemStateChanged() interface means starting with a blank template for an itemStateChanged() method, then enter the code you want to execute for the possible events that can be detected.

7. Because the state Selected for each of the radio buttons is mutually exclusive, an if ... else statement is used instead of many if statements when checking the states of the radio buttons.

8. In particular we want to know what button has been clicked. This information is obtained by using the method getSource().

Exercise 8-2

1. Write a Java program that provides a clear and simple graphical user interface for a user to supply their name, telephone number, age and gender. Use a radio button to indicate the gender.

   Implement the `itemListener` and `actionListener` interfaces so that the data entered can be used. Don't forget to register all components where user interaction is required with the relevant interface.

   Add a selection statement that will check the age and gender of the details entered. If the person is female and over 19, display the message "eligible for this course", otherwise display the message "not eligible for this course". Use a label to display the message.

2. The following JCheckBox methods can be used in your program:

`getLabel()`	returns a String containing the checkbox's label
`setLabel(String)`	Changes the check box label.
`IsSelected(boolean)`	returns true or false based on whether the check box has been selected
`setSelected(boolean)`	changes the state to selected (true) or unselected (false).

   Write a program that sets up a check box and makes use of the above methods.

3. Write a program to solve quadratic equations. Use 3 text-boxes to enter the necessary coefficients, and use labels for any prompts you feel necessary. Where are you going to store the solutions - a label may suffice.

4. A local company wants to make a start at automating their payroll system. Currently the wage packets are made up individually. They get paid in cash and have a pay receipt t hat details hours worked, rate of pay, overtime and gross pay etc.

   Assuming a basic week is 37 hours, and that any time over this is to be treated as overtime which is to be paid as 1.5 times the standard rate. Write a program that will accept input from the user for:

   Employee name, hours worked, rate of pay

   and will calculate the basic pay, tax and net pay after tax.

Chapter 9 (week 9)

Example assignment

In this chapter, I have included a simple assignment. This starts with the specification or assignment brief. There then follows a worked solution that consists mainly of program listings and screen dumps, much in the way that I would expect students to present their work. During this week they are expected to work on their assignment.

9.1 Assignment brief

Assignment for Unit 2

This assignment tests your ability to use Arrays, and create objects containing structured data. It also requires that you create a simple graphics user interface.

Task 1

This task will test that you can write a simple program that uses arrays.

A level grades are awarded as follows:

Grade A	80-100 %
Grade B	70-79 %
Grade C	60-69%
Grade D	50-59%
Grade E	40-49%
Unclassified	0- 39%

The following test data is to be used for task 1 and task 2.

```
34   47   82   23   76   45   65    9   56   37
73   67   54   49   55   44   42   75   36   53
```

(a) Write a program that allows a user to enter the above data using a keyboard and will then store it in an array. Save the program as Task1.java.

(b) Add some code to the program called Task1 so that the contents of the array are displayed on the screen. Don't forget to save the program.

(c) Extend this program, so that the last part of the program will calculate the frequency of each grade and display the results in the form of a table. Save this program again.

Task 2

This task will test your ability to represent data in a structure and access the objects that have this structure, by including instance data and instance methods

(a) Write a program that contains a class called Marks. This class should contain the following instance data:

Name, mathsMark, physicsMark, computingMark

The following data is an indication of the data to be stored in your Marks objects.

```
Colmerauer, A   92   37   65
Hopper, G       73   56   45
Kemeny, J       78   56   45
Kernighan, D    56   59   83
Ritchie, D      60   78   89
Stroustrup, B   49   64   76
Wirth, N        87   74   82
```

(b) Extend this program to include a method that will allow you to enter the details of a single Marks object from the keyboard.

(c) Create a number of constructors. One of these should allow you to initialize an object with all the instance data.

(d) Create additional methods that will allow you to display a Marks object, and another one to change the marks.

(e) Create a class called Task2 that is used as a driver program. That is, it contains the method `main()` and is used to call the methods and constructors defined in the class Marks. This driver program should create 7 Marks objects using the data in the table above. All of the methods required need to be tested by at least one method call.

Task 3

This task will test your ability to create a simple graphical user interface.

The current community charge for a given property in the London borough of Croydon, can be determined from the table below. The **total community charge** for a year is the sum of **Croydon Services** and **GLA** charge.

Amount of Council tax for the year 2002/2003

Valuation Band	Croydon Services	GLA
A	453.10	115.92
B	528.62	135.24
C	604.13	154.56
D	679.65	173.88
E	830.68	212.52
F	981.72	251.16
G	1132.75	289.80
H	1358.30	347.76

You are required to use the above information in the assignment.

Write a program that will contain the following features:

1. Use a label to display the prompt "Enter your valuation band (A – H)".

2. Create a group of 8 radio buttons corresponding to the valuation bands A – H.

3. When a user clicks on a radio button corresponding to their valuation band, the program will determine the appropriate charges for Croydon Services, and GLA. It will then calculate the Council tax which is determined by summing these two charges.

4. Finally, Display the following on the screen. Use labels to do this.

   - The valuation band entered
   - The charge for Croydon Services
   - The charge for GLA
   - The total council tax to be paid

9.2　　Task 1 solution

Example 71

```java
import java.util.Scanner;

public class Task1
{

    public static void main(String args[])
    {
        Scanner input = new Scanner(System.in);

        int marks[] = new int [20];

        // Store 20 numbers in array
        System.out.println("Entering numbers from keyboard");

        for(int i = 0; i < 20; i++)
        {
            System.out.print("Enter next number : ");
            marks[i] = input.nextInt();
        }

        //  Display contents of array
        System.out.println("The numbers stored are");
        for(int i = 0; i < 20; i++)
            System.out.print(marks[i] + "\t");
        System.out.println("");

        // Determine frequency for each grade
        int a = 0, b = 0, c = 0, d = 0, e = 0, u = 0;
        for(int i = 0; i < 20; i++)
            if (marks[i] >= 80)
                a++;
            else if (marks[i] >= 70 && marks[i] < 80)
                b++;
            else if (marks[i] >= 60 && marks[i] < 70)
                c++;
            else if (marks[i] >= 50 && marks[i] < 60)
                d++;
            else if (marks[i] >= 40 && marks[i] < 50)
                e++;
            else
                u++;

        // display frequency of grades
        System.out.println("grade\tfrequency");
        System.out.println("A\t" + a);
        System.out.println("B\t" + b);
        System.out.println("C\t" + c);
        System.out.println("D\t" + d);
```

```
        System.out.println("E\t" + e);
        System.out.println("U\t" + u);
    }
}
```

Screen dump

```
E:\JavaDev>java Task1
Entering numbers from keyboard
Enter next number : 34
Enter next number : 47
Enter next number : 82
Enter next number : 23
Enter next number : 76
Enter next number : 45
Enter next number : 65
Enter next number : 9
Enter next number : 56
Enter next number : 37
Enter next number : 73
Enter next number : 67
Enter next number : 54
Enter next number : 49
Enter next number : 55
Enter next number : 44
Enter next number : 42
Enter next number : 75
Enter next number : 36
Enter next number : 53
The numbers stored are
34        47        82        23        76        45        65        9        56        37
73        67        54        49        55        44        42        75        36        53

grade     frequency
A         1
B         3
C         2
D         4
E         5
U         5

E:\JavaDev>_
```

9.3　　　Task 2 solution

<u>Example 72</u>

```java
import java.util.Scanner;

class Marks
{
    //instance data
    private String name;
    private int maths, physics, computing;

    //constructors

    Marks()
    { name = "Unknowm"; maths = 0; physics = 0; computing = 0;}

    Marks(String n, int m, int p, int c)
    {
        name = n;
        maths = m;
        physics = p;
        computing = c;
    }

    //instance methods

    void enterDetails()
    {
        Scanner input = new Scanner(System.in);

        System.out.print("Enter name : ");
        name = input.nextLine();

        System.out.print("Enter maths mark : ");
        maths = input.nextInt();

        System.out.print("Enter physics mark : ");
        physics = input.nextInt();

        System.out.print("Enter computing mark : ");
        computing = input.nextInt();

        System.out.println("");
    }


    void showDetails()
    {
        System.out.println("Name            : " + name);
        System.out.println("Maths mark      : " + maths);
        System.out.println("Physics mark    : " + physics);
        System.out.println("Computing mark : " + computing);
```

```java
            System.out.println("");
        }

    void changeMarks()
    {
            Scanner input = new Scanner(System.in);

            System.out.println("Change marks for " + name);

            System.out.println("Current maths mark is : " + maths);
            System.out.print("Enter new maths mark : ");
            maths = input.nextInt();

            System.out.println("Current physics mark is : " +
                                physics);
            System.out.print("Enter physics mark : ");
            physics = input.nextInt();

            System.out.println("Current computing mark is : " +
                                computing);
            System.out.print("Enter computing mark : ");
            computing = input.nextInt();

            System.out.println("");
        }
}

public class Task2
{
    public static void main(String args[])
    {
            Marks a = new Marks("Colmerauer, A", 92, 37, 65);
            a.showDetails();

            Marks b = new Marks("Hopper, G", 73, 56, 45);
            b.showDetails();

            Marks c = new Marks("Kemeny, J", 78, 56, 45);
            c.showDetails();

            Marks d = new Marks("Kernighan, D", 56, 59, 83);
            d.showDetails();

            Marks e = new Marks("Ritchie, D", 56, 59, 83);
            e.showDetails();

            Marks f = new Marks();
            f.enterDetails();
            f.showDetails();

            Marks g = new Marks();
            g.enterDetails();
            g.showDetails();
```

```
        g.changeMarks();
        g.showDetails();

    }
}
```

Screen dump

```
 cmd

E:\JavaDev>java Task2
Name            : Colmerauer, A
Maths mark      : 92
Physics mark    : 37
Computing mark  : 65

Name            : Hopper, G
Maths mark      : 73
Physics mark    : 56
Computing mark  : 45

Name            : Kemeny, J
Maths mark      : 78
Physics mark    : 56
Computing mark  : 45

Name            : Kernighan, D
Maths mark      : 56
Physics mark    : 59
Computing mark  : 83

Name            : Ritchie, D
Maths mark      : 56
Physics mark    : 59
Computing mark  : 83

Enter name : Stroustrup, B
Enter maths mark : 49
Enter physics mark : 64
Enter computing mark : 76

Name            : Stroustrup, B
Maths mark      : 49
Physics mark    : 64
Computing mark  : 76

Enter name : Wirth, N
Enter maths mark : 87
Enter physics mark : 74
Enter computing mark : 82

Name            : Wirth, N
Maths mark      : 87
Physics mark    : 74
Computing mark  : 82

Change marks for Wirth, N
Current maths mark is : 87
Enter new maths mark : 65
Current physics mark is : 74
Enter physics mark : 78
Current computing mark is : 82
Enter computing mark : 65

Name            : Wirth, N
Maths mark      : 65
Physics mark    : 78
Computing mark  : 65


E:\JavaDev>
```

9.4 Task 3 solution

<u>Example 73</u>

```java
import javax.swing.*;
import java.awt.*;
import java.awt.event.*;

public class Task3 extends JFrame
{
    private JLabel VBprompt, VBsummary, CSsummary, GLAsummary, CTsummary;
    private JRadioButton a, b, c, d, e, f, g, h;
    double CroyService, GLA, councilTax;
    private ButtonGroup valBand;
    private Container contents;

    public Task3(String s)
    {
        super(s);
        contents = getContentPane();

        setSize(400, 200);
        contents.setLayout(new FlowLayout());

        //Create label for Valution band prompt
        VBprompt = new JLabel("Enter your valuation band (A - H)   "
                        + "                              "
                        + "                             ");
        contents.add(VBprompt);

        //Create radio buttons
        a = new JRadioButton("A");
        b = new JRadioButton("B");
        c = new JRadioButton("C");
        d = new JRadioButton("D");
        e = new JRadioButton("E");
        f = new JRadioButton("F");
        g = new JRadioButton("G");
        h = new JRadioButton("H");

        //add radio buttons to Frame
        contents.add(a); contents.add(b);
        contents.add(c); contents.add(d);
        contents.add(e); contents.add(f);
        contents.add(g); contents.add(h);

        //Create Radio button group
        valBand = new ButtonGroup();
        valBand.add(a); valBand.add(b);
        valBand.add(c); valBand.add(d);
        valBand.add(e); valBand.add(f);
        valBand.add(g); valBand.add(h);

        //Create TestRadioButton event handler object
        TestRadioButton trb = new TestRadioButton();
        //Register event handler with checkboxes
        a.addItemListener(trb); b.addItemListener(trb);
```

```
        c.addItemListener(trb); d.addItemListener(trb);
        e.addItemListener(trb); f.addItemListener(trb);
        g.addItemListener(trb); h.addItemListener(trb);

        //Add label for valuation band summary
        VBsummary = new JLabel();
        contents.add(VBsummary);

        //Add label for Croydon Services summary
        CSsummary = new JLabel();
        contents.add(CSsummary);

        //Add label for GLA summary
        GLAsummary = new JLabel();
        contents.add(GLAsummary);

        //Add label for Council tax summary
        CTsummary = new JLabel();
        contents.add(CTsummary);

        setVisible(true);
    }

private class TestRadioButton implements ItemListener
{
    public void itemStateChanged(ItemEvent ie)
    {
      //Check each checkbox for a change of state
      if (ie.getSource() == a)
      {
            VBsummary.setText("The valuation band chosen is A");
            CroyService = 453.10;
            GLA = 115.92;
      }
      else if (ie.getSource() == b)
      {
            VBsummary.setText("The valuation band chosen is B");
            CroyService = 528.62;
            GLA = 135.24;
      }
      else if (ie.getSource() == c)
      {
            VBsummary.setText("The valuation band chosen is C");
            CroyService = 604.13;
            GLA = 154.56;
      }
      else if (ie.getSource() == d)
      {
            VBsummary.setText("The valuation band chosen is D");
            CroyService = 679.65;
            GLA = 173.88;
      }
      else if (ie.getSource() == e)
      {
            VBsummary.setText("The valuation band chosen is E");
            CroyService = 830.68;
            GLA = 212.52;
      }
```

```
        else if (ie.getSource() == f)
        {
                VBsummary.setText("The valuation band chosen is F");
                CroyService = 981.72;
                GLA = 251.15;
        }
        else if (ie.getSource() == g)
        {
                VBsummary.setText("The valuation band chosen is F");
                CroyService = 289.80;
                GLA = 289.80;
        }
        else if (ie.getSource() == h)
        {
                VBsummary.setText("The valuation band chosen is H");
                CroyService = 1138.30;
                GLA = 347.76;
        }

        CSsummary.setText("The charge for Croydon services is " +
                        CroyService);
        GLAsummary.setText("The charge for GLA is " + GLA);
        councilTax = CroyService + GLA;
        CTsummary.setText("The total charge for Council Tax is " +
                        councilTax);
    }
}

    public static void main(String args [])
    {
        Task3 t3 = new Task3("Radio button demo");
    }
}
```

Screen dump

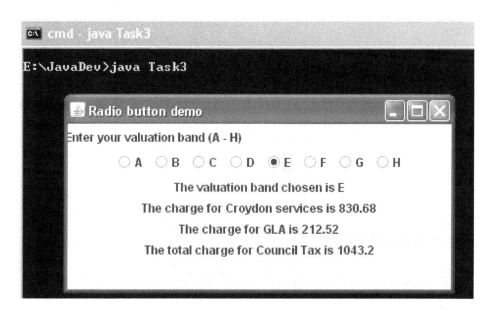

Chapter 10 (Week 10)

This week will be set aside to complete the assignment. It may also be used to consolidate material. You could start by reading the end of unit summary.

10.1   Tasks to finish

This week is to be used to finish your coursework. At this stage you should have all the skills that you need to complete your coursework. I will include a basic list of tasks that will summarise what you need to do.

Part 2 of the book follows on where part one left off. You will have to retain the knowledge and skills gained in part one of the book, as many of the ideas will be required to carry out the tasks for the assignment set for this unit.

In addition there are a lot of new topics that you will have to be familiar with. In particular you will notice that you are expected to write longer programs, so that it is only sensible to write methods to do a number of the tasks. The use of methods in your program not only reduces the amount of code you may have to type, it makes it easier to correct and maintain.

The tasks that you will be asked to do have been broken down into small stages. It is recommended that you write your programs bit by bit as suggested by the example assignment in the previous chapter. If you write programs in this manner, it will be much easier to spot and correct errors when they occur, as you will only be writing a small amount of code each time before compiling and running it.

You will have to understand the basic idea of arrays. In this book the subject has been treated very simply. You have just been told enough to get on and write the programs that you need to.

There is a chapter which covers classes and objects. most of this is there just to help you understand what you are doing when you use existing Java classes. It is really preparing you for what is one of the most difficult topics covered in this book. Namely creating graphical user interfaces GUIs that a user can interact with when they are running your Java application. Graphical User Interfaces will also be used in part 3 of the book, but in the context of writing applets.

10.2   End of Unit Summary

1. An array is a sequential collection of like data. This data can consist of one of the 8 primitive data types within Java, or can be an object.

2. Each element of an array is accessed using the name of an array and an index. The index is a number that refers to the relative position within an array.

3. The index of the first element is 0, the second is 1 and so on.

4. It is quite common for each element of and array to be accessed when they are processed. It is for this reason that for loops are most commonly used.

5. Arrays are created as objects. They are similar to arrays in C and C++, but also have instance data. In particular each array has a variable called length.

6. This variable called length can be used when you are processing array. You can use it to tell where the last element is.

7. If you use this value in a for loop, there is much less chance of reading past the end of an array.

8. A method is a self-contained unit of code that can be executed many times. In other languages such as C or C++ they are usually referred to as functions.

9. A method definition consists of a method header and a method body. The header consists of a name, a list of parameters and their type, and the type of the return value.

10. The method body contains the code that is to be executed. It consists of one or more Java statements.

11. The method is executed whenever there appears a method call in the program. A method call consists of the method name followed by list of parameter values contained within round brackets ().

12. It is possible that the return value is of type void. If this is the case, nothing is returned. Instead, it is usually the case that the method is being used to just output something on the screen – not carry out a calculation.

13. A recursive method is a method that is self-referential – that is it refers to itself. That is a recursive method will contain method calls to itself. When you write a recursive function, it does one of two things, it either calls itself or terminates. It is most important that you write a selection statement that can determine when the recursive method will terminate.

14. If you fill a large array, it is most important that you are able to search for a particular value. The simplest type of search is called a linear search. This involves starting at the beginning of the array, and inspect each element until you find the value you are looking for.

15. A linear search can be very slow, as the length of the search, and hence time taken is proportional to the size of the array.

16. A much better method is to use a bisection search.

17. If you want to search an array, it is important that the array is sorted.

18. The simplest type of sort algorithm to implement is called a bubble sort. Unfortunately it is also very slow. Fortunately there are more efficient sorting algorithms, but this is beyond the scope of this book.

19. Java is an object-oriented language as the program itself is a class.

20. A class is composed of member data and member functions called methods.

21. A class method is identified by the word static.

22. All other methods are called instance methods. Typically all instance methods require an object of this class-type to call them.

23. There is a special category of instance methods called constructors. They have the same name as the class, and are used to construct new objects.

24. Access modifiers are used within a class to specify the type of access that member data and methods have.

25. Java provides powerful facilities for creating graphical user interfaces (GUIs).

26. The AWT and swing packages are used to create GUIs.

27. These packages provide graphics utilities, GUI components and layout managers.

28. Swing is a later development, and is built on the AWT class. It has newer GUI components that can be made to look the same no matter what type of computer environment it is running on.

29. The GUI components include: labels, text boxes, text areas, buttons, check-buttons, radio buttons and choice lists.

30. The 3 main layout managers described in this book are: FlowLayout, GridLayout and BorderLayout.

31. You can get GUI components to interact with a user. They use an event-driven model.

32. To make a component able to interact with a user, you need to implement a listener interface.

33. This involves stating that the class implements the listener interface you are to use, adding code to a blank interface method to specify the actions to be carried out, and registering all components involved with the listener interface.

Part 3

Programming for the Internet using applets

Aims

After completing this 5-week unit, you will be able to do the following:

Introduction to applets and graphics

Write simple applets using an editor such as notepad.

Run applets using `appletviewer` and also from a web page.

Understand the applet life-cycle.

Write programs that use 2D graphics.

Data

Write Java applets that include a range of Java data types. This should include declaration of variables and variable assignment.

Use different arithmetic operators and predefined mathematical methods available in the Math class to carry out computation.

Input and output

Write simple working applets that include suitable input – use input dialog boxes.

Use the `paint()` method for displaying output.

Control structures

Use appropriate selection methods to solve particular programming problems.

Use appropriate iteration methods. These should include both definite and indefinite loops.

Methods and arrays

Write one or more applets that use an array

Write one or more applets that use user-defined methods.

Graphical User Interfaces (GUI)

Use the awt and swing packages to implement a simple Graphical User Interface (GUI) within an applet.

Include such GUI components as labels, text fields, text areas, buttons, radio buttons, check boxes and drop-down menus.

Use layout managers – FlowLayout, BorderLayout and GridLayout, to allow you to add several components.

Implement an event handler so that a user can interact with the components.

Chapter 11 (week 11)

Using applets and some simple graphics

11.1   Introducing applets

An applet is a Java program that is typically run from a web page (HTML file). They can also be run using **appletviewer** – part of the Sun JDK. Appletviewer is mostly used when developing and testing Java applets. This is the case, as you can obtain additional information when you run the applet using appletviewer.

The process of creating an applet involves the following:

1. Write a Java applet program and compile it using javac. If there are no errors this will create a Java class file.

2. Write an HTML file that links to the Java class file.

3. Run the appletviewer program, using the name of the HTML file as a parameter.

4. If the result of running appletviewer is successful, you know that you can run the applet from a web page.

We will be creating applets using the JApplet class which is part of the swing package. It is for this reason we will always use:

```
Import javax.swing.JApplet;
```

Or the more general

```
Import javax.swing.*;
```

when we want to use other facilities within the swing package as well.

We will not as a general rule use the older Applet class to be found in the awt package.

When we come to write the applet, the class is defined so that it inherits properties from the JApplet class. Inheriting properties from another class in this way, means that the methods of that class are made available to the program.

There are two important methods that we will be using all the time. They are `init()` and `paint()`. The `init()` method is run when the applet starts. It is used for initialization.   The `paint()` method is used to display text on the screen, and also to plot graphics objects. You will notice that the `paint()` method takes a single parameter of type Graphics. The Graphics class is part of the awt package, and is used to determine the colour of both text and graphics objects. Also, it contains methods that enable us to provide output. In particular the first method that we will be using, that needs a Graphics object to call it is `drawString()`. This is used to output a string to a certain position.

11.2   Creating and running applets

Applets are derived from the JApplet class and have to be compiled in the same way as Java applications. Unlike a Java application an applet needs to be run from a browser - and so will need an html file which references the .class file.

The following code is an example of a very simple applet.

Example 74

```java
import javax.swing.JApplet;
import java.awt.*;

public class App1 extends JApplet
{
    Font f = new Font("SansSerif", Font.BOLD, 36);

    public void paint(Graphics g)
    {
      g.setFont(f);
      g.setColor(Color.green);
      g.drawString("This text is green and is", 5, 40);
      g.drawString("printed in Sans Serif bold", 5, 80);
    }
}
```

The above source code is compiled with the command:

```
javac App1.java
```

to produce a class file called App1.class.

To run the contents of the class file, we need an html file that references it.

Example 75

```
<Head>
<Title>Test Applet</Title>
</Head>
<Body>
    Output from applet
    <P><Applet code = "App1.class" Width = 500 Height = 200>
        </Applet>
    </P>
</Body>
```

The applet can now be run using AppletViewer by entering the following command:

```
appletviewer App1.html
```

Alternatively the applet can be run using your web browser. In the example shown, the html file has been opened using Internet Explorer.

177

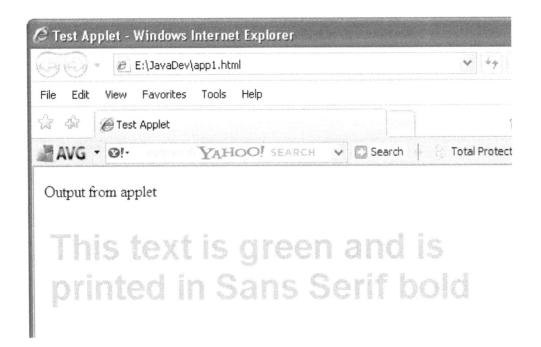

Notes:

1. All applet classes must extend the JApplet class.

2. The **JApplet** class is defined in **javax.swing.JApplet**. The inclusion of the statement **import javax.swing.*;** allows you to access all the classes in this package. One such class is JApplet.

3. The statement **import java.awt.*;** allows access to the **Graphics** class. We need this to use the method paint().

4. The paint() method needs to be overridden if you wish to print text or draw within the applet window.

5. paint() always has one parameter - an object of type Graphics.

6. drawString() is used to plot text on the screen. It needs an object of type Graphics to call it.

7. The code g.drawString() method uses an **(x, y)** coordinate system, where the numbers represent pixels on the screen.

8. The <Applet> tag in the HTML file is used to specify the class file of the applet to be run. The Height and Width qualifiers specify the size of the space to be allocated.

11.3 The applet life-cycle

Unlike Java applications, which have a method called `main()` which executes when a program is run, applets have many methods which are run depending on various events that may occur during an applets life-cycle.

The methods provided in the applet class for each activity typically do nothing. It is up to the programmer to override them if they wish something to occur.

Some of the main methods are described:

`init()`   is executed when the applet is first loaded or reloaded

`start()`   is executed immediately after `init()` has run. It can be executed many times, particularly if the applet has been stopped. It starts again when the user returns to the web page.

`stop()`   an applet stops when the reader leaves the web page.

`destroy()` This method releases resources and cleans up. This method is typically is not overridden.

The following program demonstrates these methods:

Example 76

```
import javax.swing.*;
import java.awt.*;

public class AppLifeCycle extends JApplet
{
   int initCnt = 0;
   int startCnt = 0;
   int stopCnt = 0;
   int destroyCnt = 0;

   public void init()
   {
      ++initCnt;
      System.out.println("init() has executed " + initCnt + "times");
   }

   public void start()
   {
      ++startCnt;
      System.out.println("start() has executed " + startCnt + "times");
   }

   public void stop()
   {
      ++stopCnt;
      System.out.println("stop() has executed " + stopCnt + "times");
   }
```

```
   public void destroy()
   {
      ++destroyCnt;
      System.out.println("destroy() has executed " + destroyCnt +
                              " times");
   }
}
```

As you can see from the screen dump below you can stop and start the applet.

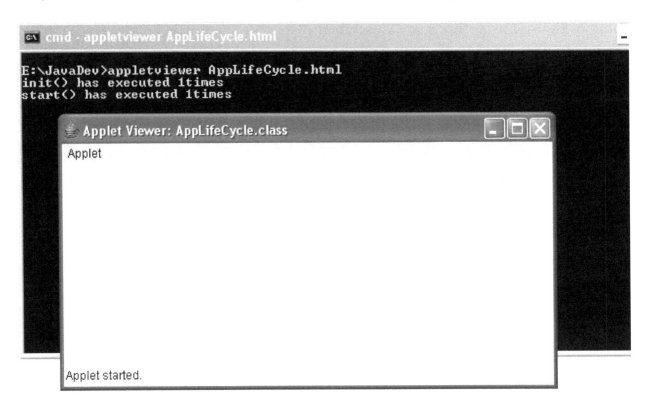

You can close the applet by clicking on the minimize button. If you close and open the applet a number of times you can obtain the following:

```
E:\JavaDev>appletviewer AppLifeCycle.html
init() has executed 1times
start() has executed 1times
stop() has executed 1times
start() has executed 2times
stop() has executed 2times
start() has executed 3times
```

In addition to the methods described, you will also need to use the `paint()` method. This is required for all output to the screen. This can include displaying text and simple graphics.

11.3 Simple graphics

Graphics operations are done within the method `paint()` which has one parameter - an object of type Graphics. It is this Graphics object that is used to call Graphics methods to draw in the applet.

The co-ordinate system for an applet panel is as follows:

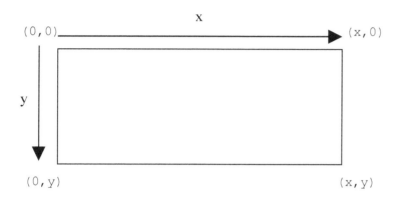

11.3.1 Drawing a line

Example 77

```java
import javax.swing.JApplet;
import java.awt.*;

public class Line extends JApplet
{
    public void paint(Graphics g)
    {
        int x1 = 100, y1 = 50, x2 = 50, y2 = 80;
        g.drawLine(x1, y1, x2, y2);
        g.drawString("(100,50)", x1, y1);
        g.drawString("(50,80)", x2, y2);
    }
}
```

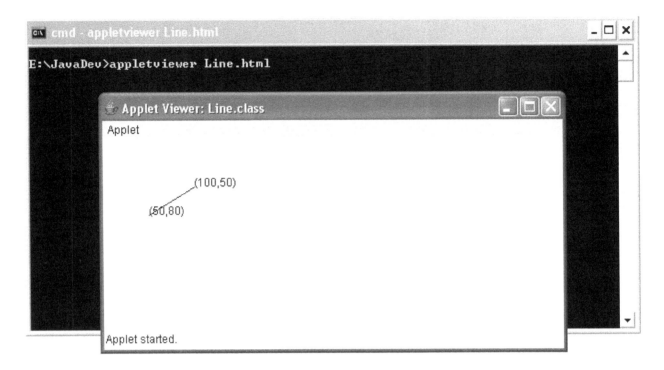

Notes:

1. The object g is of type Graphics. It is used to call the `drawLine()` and `drawString()` methods.

2. The `drawLine()` method takes 4 parameters. These 4 values specify the two end-points of the line

3. The `drawString()` method writes the string within the quotes, starting at position x, y.

11.3.2 Drawing a rectangle

<u>Example 78</u>

```java
import javax.swing.JApplet;
import java.awt.*;

public class rect extends JApplet
{
    public void paint(Graphics g)
    {
        int w1 = 100, h1 = 50, w2 = 50, h2 = 80;
        g.drawRect(50, 50, w1, h1);
        g.fillRect(200, 50, w2, h2);
    }
}
```

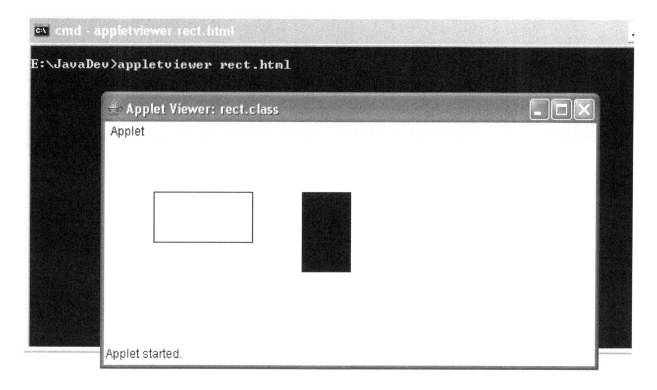

Notes:

1. `drawRect()` has 4 parameters. The first two locate the top left-hand corner. The last two specify the width and height.

2. `fillRect()` has the same format as `drawRect()` - but this time you get a filled rectangle.

11.3.3   Drawing an oval

Example 79

```
import javax.swing.JApplet;
import java.awt.*;

public class Oval extends JApplet
{
    public void paint(Graphics g)
    {
        int w1 = 100, h1 = 50, w2 = 50, h2 = 80;
        g.drawRect(50, 50, w1, h1);
        g.drawOval(50, 50, w1, h1);
        g.drawRect(200, 50, w2, h2);
        g.fillOval(200, 50, w2, h2);
    }
}
```

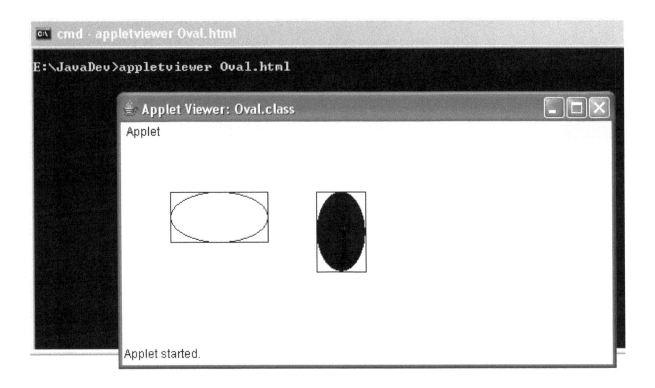

Notes:

1. `drawOval()` and `fillOval()` have the same format as the `drawRect()` and `fillRect()` methods.

2. The method `drawOval()` is used to draw the outline of an oval, and `fillOval()` is used to draw a filled oval.

3. Like a rectangle, an oval requires 4 parameters. The parameters to be used are exactly those for a rectangle that would enclose the oval and touch on four sides.

4. The above program demonstrates this by plotting ovals within an equivalent rectangle.

11.3.4　Drawing a polygon

Example 80

```
import javax.swing.JApplet;
import java.awt.*;

public class Polygon extends JApplet
{
    public void paint(Graphics g)
    {
        int x[] = {50, 100, 125, 100, 50, 25};
        int y[] = {7, 7, 50, 93, 93, 50};
        int x2[] = {250, 300, 325, 300, 250, 225};
```

```
            g.drawPolygon(x, y, 6);
            g.fillPolygon(x2,y, 6);
        }
    }
```

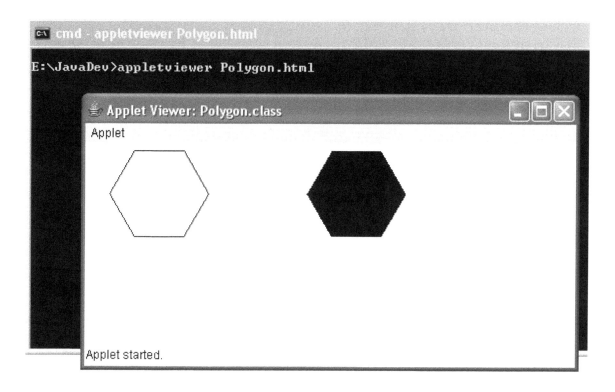

Notes:

1. The `drawPolygon()` method requires 3 parameters. The first two parameters , x and y are arrays of type int. These are used to store a list of x and y co-ordinates, representing the corners of the polygon. The third parameter is the number of sides or corners.

2. The `fillPolygon()` is similar to the `drawPolygon()`. It too requires 3 parameters. Unlike `drawPolygon()`, it draws a filled polygon.

11.3.5   Drawing an arc

Example 81

```
import javax.swing.JApplet;
import java.awt.*;

public class Arc extends JApplet
{
    public void paint(Graphics g)
    {
        g.drawArc(10,10,100,100,0,90);          // (a)
        g.drawString("(a)",10,50);
        g.fillArc(120,10,100,100,0,90);         // (b)
        g.drawString("(b)",120,50);
        g.drawArc(240,10,100,100,-45,90);       // (c)
```

```
        g.drawString("(c)",240,50);
        g.fillArc(380,10,100,100,60,120);          // (d)
        g.drawString("(d)",360,50);
        g.drawArc(10,120,100,60,0,180);            // (e)
        g.drawString("(e)",10,160);
        g.fillArc(120,120,80,50,-135,180);         // (f)
        g.drawString("(f)",120,160);
    }
}
```

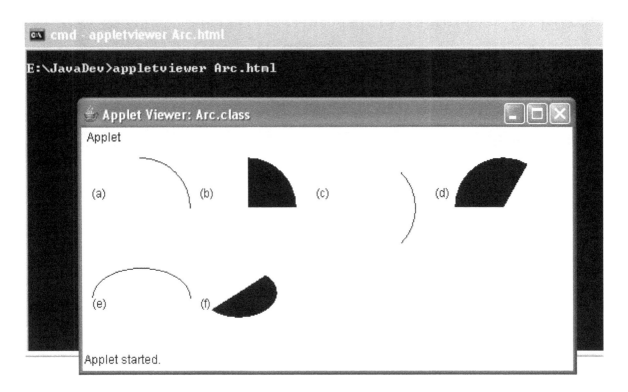

Notes:

1. A simple arc is plotted using `drawArc()` - it is similar to the `drawOval()` method.

2. It has two more parameters than the method `drawOval()`. These extra parameters specify an angle in degrees for the start of the arc, and then an angle in degrees to indicate the size of the arc.

Exercise 11-1

1. Write a program to draw the following cube. Use two different versions. One which uses only lines, and another which uses rectangles and lines.

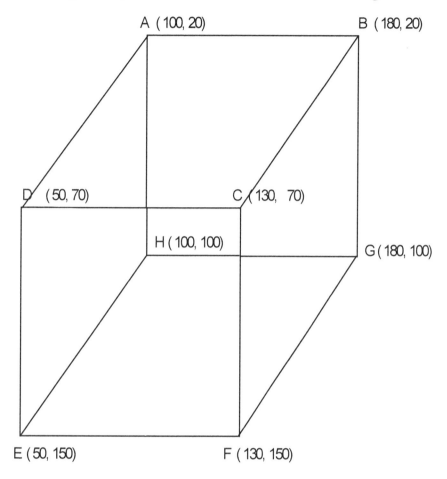

A (100, 20) B (180, 20)
D (50, 70) C (130, 70)
H (100, 100) G (180, 100)
E (50, 150) F (130, 150)

2 (a) Write a program to simulate the operation of a set of traffic lights such as the following:

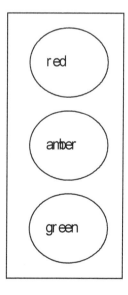

(b) Introduce a delay of several seconds in between the lights changing. This could be achieved by writing a method called delay that pauses for several seconds.

Chapter 12 (week 12)

Calculations, control structures and methods

In this chapter we will be looking at concepts that have already been covered in parts 1 and 2 of this book. They will however be used in the writing of Java applets, rather than Java applications. Only those concepts previously not explained will be explained here in any detail.

12.1 Calculate results from expressions

Here is another version of the temp program. It was copied from unit 2, and modified so that it can be run as an applet.

Example 82

```java
import javax.swing.*;
import java.awt.*;

public class temp extends JApplet
{
   float c, f;

   public void init()
   {
     String temp;

     temp = JOptionPane.showInputDialog("Enter temperature"
              + " (degrees C) : ");

     c = Float.parseFloat(temp);

     f = 9/5 * c + 32;
   }

   public void paint(Graphics g)
   {
     super.paint(g);

     g.drawString("The temperature " + c + " degrees C", 5, 40);
     g.drawString("is " + f + " degrees F", 5, 60);
   }
}
```

The Input dialog box

The applet after entering a value and clicking on OK

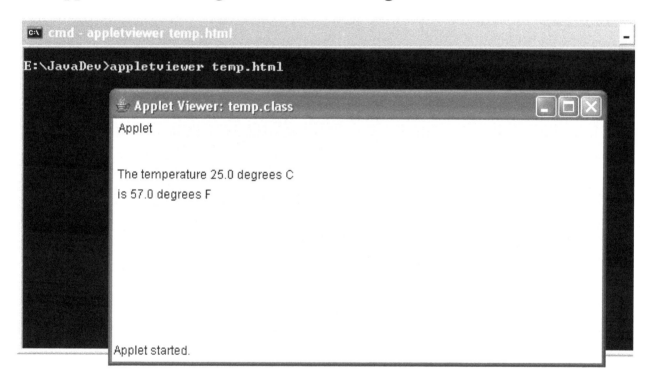

Notes:

1. The variables c and f are declared before any of the methods. Effectively they are global variables, and as such are available to both methods as they can be accessed anywhere within the class temp.

2. The **init()** method is used to do everything that does not involve displaying output. This is the first method to run and is typically used to initialize all variables. In this example we have also carried out all the required calculations.

3. The method `parseFloat()` is used to extract a float from the string. The wrapper class `Float` is needed to do this.

4. Within the `init()` method, an input dialog box is used to enter the temperature in degrees C.

5. As the input entered is treated as a string, it needs to be converted to a float. Then the calculation can be performed to obtain a temperature in degrees Fahrenheit.

6. The **paint()** method is used to perform all the output operations. In this case the method **drawString()** is used to output two strings.

12.2   Another arithmetic example

The program that follows is a longer example. It is also based on a previous example that has been adapted to run as an applet.

Example 83

```
import javax.swing.*;
import java.awt.*;

public class quad extends JApplet
{
    int a, b, c;              //3 quadratic coefficients
    double x1, x2;    //2 roots

    Font f = new Font("SansSerif", Font.BOLD, 24);

    public void init()
    {
      //Enter coefficients
      String a_string = JOptionPane.showInputDialog
      ("Enter coefficient a : ");
      a = Integer.parseInt(a_string);

      String b_string = JOptionPane.showInputDialog
      ("Enter coefficient b : ");
      b = Integer.parseInt(b_string);

      String c_string = JOptionPane.showInputDialog
      ("Enter coefficient c : ");
      c = Integer.parseInt(c_string);

      //calculation
      double d = (double) (b * b - 4 * a * c);
      double d2 = Math.sqrt(d);
      x1 = (-b + d) / (2 * a);
      x2 = (-b - d) / (2 * a);

      System.out.println("x is either " + x1 + " or " + x2);
```

```
    }

    public void paint(Graphics g)
    {
        g.setFont(f);
        g.setColor(Color.green);
        g.drawString("x = " + x1, 5, 40);
        g.drawString("or x = " + x2, 5, 60);
    }
}
```

We are required to enter 3 integers at the keyboard. Each item of data that needs to be entered requires an input dialog box. Once you have entered a value, and clicked on OK, the input dialog box is closed.

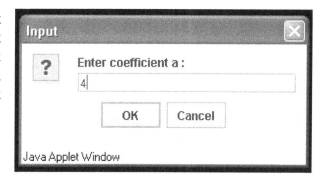

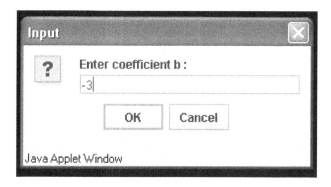
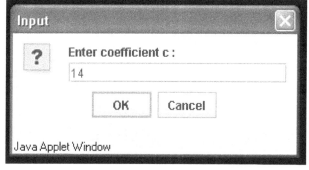

The following shows the applet when the applet has completed.

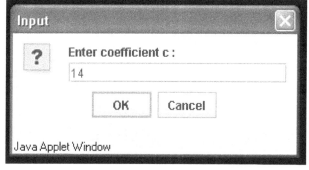

Notes:

1. As with the previous example, all of the computation where possible that does not involve output to the applet window is carried out in the method `init()`.

2. Three input dialog boxes are created - one for each of the coefficients a, b and c. This will store the numeric coefficients in the form of a string. Each of these has a prompt telling the user to type in the coefficient. Possibly, this prompt is inadequate, as it does not specify that you have to type in an integer.

3. For each string stored in a input dialog box, we will need to use the method `parseInt()` to convert the string to type int. This requires the wrapper class Integer.

4. The calculation to work out roots of the equation x1 and x2 is the same as an earlier example in the book.

5. The output using `println()` can occur in the `init()` method, as this does not take place in the applet window, it appears on the console corresponding to the window used by cmd. This output is not really required. You would only normally do this type of thing if you were testing an applet.

6. The main output is carried out using the `paint()` method. In particular here, there are two `drawString()` statements to display the results.

13.3   Using an if statement

This uses the same if statement, used in a previous program. The main difference is how the input and output is achieved as we are writing an applet.

Example 84

```java
import javax.swing.*;
import java.awt.*;

public class if1 extends JApplet
{
    Font f = new Font("SansSerif", Font.BOLD, 20);

    String n_string;
    int n;

    public void init()
    {
      n_string = JOptionPane.showInputDialog
      ("Enter a whole number : ");
      n = Integer.parseInt(n_string);
    }

    public void paint(Graphics g)
    {
      g.setFont(f);
      g.setColor(Color.green);

      if (n > 0)
         g.drawString(" number is positive ",5,40);
      else if (n < 0)
         g.drawString("number is negative", 5, 60);
      else
         g.drawString("number is zero", 5, 80);
    }
}
```

Data entry

Resulting applet

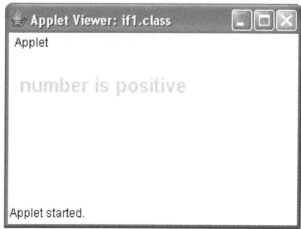

Notes:

1. In this example the method `init()` is only used to input an integer.

2. The `paint()` method contains the if statement, as the actions associated with the if statement involve output to the screen. The only place this can be done is from within the `paint()` method.

12.4   Using a switch statement

This example was based on the assignment in part 1 of the book. It has been rewritten as an applet.

Example 85

```
import javax.swing.*;
import java.awt.*;

public class switch1 extends JApplet
{
    Font f = new Font("SansSerif", Font.BOLD, 18);

    double croyService, gla, councilTax;

    char valBand;
    boolean validValBand = true;

    public void init()
    {
      //Enter valuation band
      String valStr = JOptionPane.showInputDialog
      ("Enter Valuation band (A - H) : ");
      valBand = valStr.charAt(0);

      //Select appropriate rate for Croydon services, and GLA
      switch(valBand)
      {
          case 'A':
          case 'a': croyService = 453.10; gla = 115.92;
                    break;
          case 'B':
          case 'b': croyService = 528.62; gla = 135.24;
                      break;
          case 'C':
          case 'c': croyService = 604.13; gla = 154.56;
                      break;
          case 'D':
          case 'd': croyService = 679.65; gla = 173.88;
                      break;
          case 'E':
          case 'e': croyService = 830.68; gla = 173.88;
```

194

```
                                break;
        case 'F':
        case 'f': croyService = 981.72; gla = 251.16;
                                break;
        case 'G':
        case 'g': croyService = 1132.75; gla = 289.90;
                                break;
        case 'H':
        case 'h': croyService = 1358.30; gla = 347.76;
                                break;
        default:  validValBand = false; break;
    }

    if (validValBand)
        councilTax = croyService + gla;
}

public void paint(Graphics g)
{
  g.setFont(f);
  g.setColor(Color.DARK_GRAY);
  if (validValBand)
  {
      g.drawString("The valuation Band entered is   " +
      valBand, 5, 20);
      g.drawString("The Croydon Services charge is " +
      croyService, 5, 40);
      g.drawString("The gla charge is              " +
      gla, 5, 60);
      g.drawString("The total council tax is       " +
      councilTax, 5, 80);
  }
  else
      g.drawString("An invalid valuation band was entered",
      5, 20);
  }
}
```

Input dialog box

195

Applet

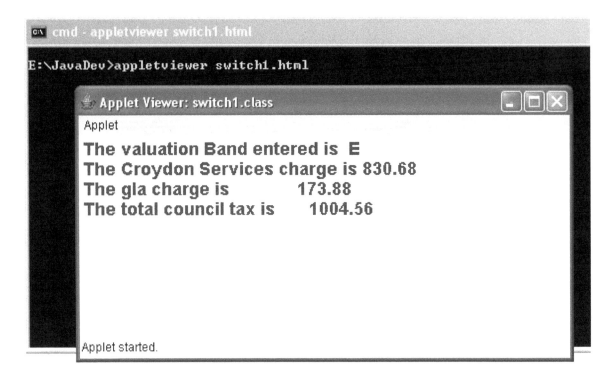

Notes:

1. In this example, the bulk of the code is contained within the `init()` method. Here a value is entered for the valuation band using an input dialog box.

2. A large switch statement is used to compare the value of the valuation band. When a match is found for a given value of valBand, the variables croyService and gla are assigned numerical values.

3. If the switch statement fails to find a match, the default action is performed. In this case a flag is used to indicate the valuation band entered is not valid. Setting validValBand to false indicates that the value entered was not within the range of values required.

4. The flag validValBand can be used in an if statement. If false, we know that there is no point doing any calculations.

5. The `paint()` method is used to provide the output. Firstly, an if statement is used to determine whether there is any point displaying any output. If the flag validValBand has been set to false, this would indicate that no calculation has been performed, an hence there is no reason to provide output.

12.5   An introduction to iteration

There are many programming problems that require the same sequence of statements to be executed again and again, either a fixed number of times or an indefinite number of times. One way to do this would be to type in the same code many times. However, this is very impractical, especially if the code needs to be repeated many times. Also, we don't always know in advance how many times the statements are to be repeated.

The repeated execution of the same statements is often called looping (or iteration). If the number of repetitions is known in advance, the **for** statement is probably the most appropriate to use.

In all other situations, either **do** or **while** statements should be used.

For this, and the sections on iteration that follow, refer back to chapter 3 where there are more examples. Note in chapter 3, everything is done in the context of an application rather than an applet.

12.6   Looping a fixed number of times

Example 86

```java
// Compute and print out a multiplication table

import javax.swing.*;
import java.awt.*;

public class mult extends JApplet
{
    int n, total = 0;

    Font f = new Font("SansSerif", Font.BOLD, 24);

    public void init()
    {
        String number;
        number = JOptionPane.showInputDialog
        ("You are about to sum an arithmetic series\n" +
          "How many terms : ");
        n = Integer.parseInt(number);

        for(int c = 1; c <= n; c++)
            total += c;
    }

    public void paint(Graphics g)
    {
        g.setFont(f);
        g.setColor(Color.DARK_GRAY);

        g.drawString("The sum of the first " + n + " integers is "
                    + total, 5, 20);
    }
}
```

Input dialog box

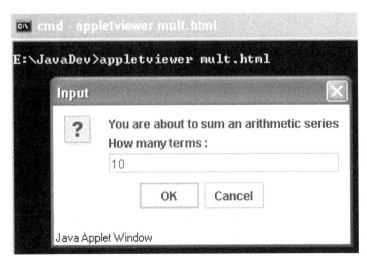

198

Resulting applet

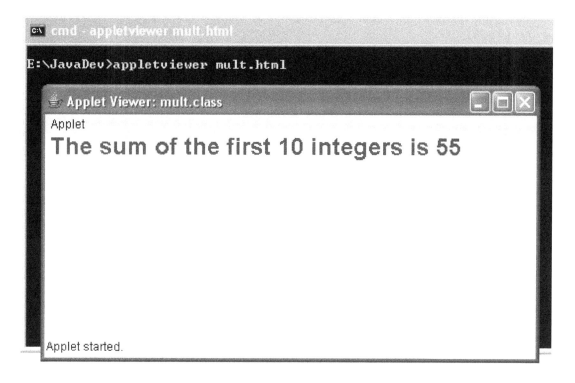

Notes:

1. In this example, we are required to add a number of numbers that are to typed in at the keyboard.

2. Two integers are declared before the loop – n and total. The variable n is used to store the quantity of numbers to be entered, and total is used to store the current total. They are declared outside both methods, so they are effectively global, and can be accessed by both methods.

3. The variable total needs to be initialized. It is assigned a value of 0, as this is what we would expect the total to be before of the numbers are added up.

4. All of the input using an input dialog box each time, is carried out within the `init()` method. The first time this happens, the user indicates how many numbers are to be entered.

5. This value is used to terminate the for loop used. An explanation of how the for loop works has already been covered in previous sections of the book.

6. Each time a number is input it is added to the current total. When the for loop has finished executing, the value stored in total will represent the sum of the numbers.

7. The `paint()` method is used to output the results.

12.7   The while loop

<u>Example 87</u>

```java
// Compute average of a set of numbers terminated by -1

import javax.swing.*;
import java.awt.*;

public class varloop extends JApplet
{
    Font font = new Font("SansSerif", Font.BOLD, 24);

    int c = 0;
    double n = 0.0, total = 0.0, average;

    public void init()
    {
      while (n != -1)
      {
            String number = JOptionPane.showInputDialog
            ("Enter next number (terminate with -1) :");
            n = Double.parseDouble(number);

            if (n != -1.0) { total += n; c++; }
      }

      average = total / c;
    }

    public void paint(Graphics g)
    {
      g.setFont(font);
      g.setColor(Color.DARK_GRAY);
      g.drawString(c + " numbers were entered", 5, 40);
      g.drawString("The total is is " + total, 5, 80);
      g.drawString("The average is " + average, 5, 120);
    }
}
```

Input dialog box

200

Applet

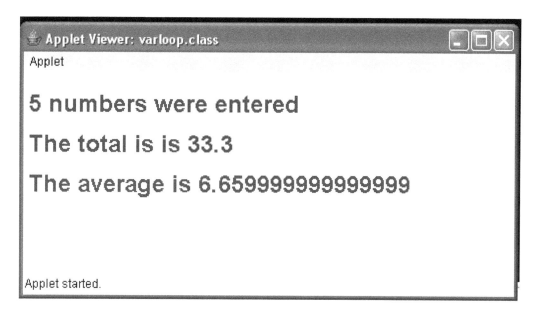

Notes:

1. In this example, a rogue value (− 1) is used to terminate the loop .

2. As before, all variables are declared as global variables. They are also given an initial value of zero. The variable n is also given a value of zero. Why? I have chosen to do this to make sure that it cannot possibly have a value of − 1, because if it did, the loop would terminate immediately.

3. Within the loop, a number is entered using an input dialog box. If this number is not −1, it is added to the total. An if statement makes sure that this is the case. Also, the variable c is incremented by 1. The variable c is being used as a counter. It counts how many numbers have been added to the total.

4. The loop terminates when a value of −1 is entered. The average is then computed by dividing the total by the count of the number of numbers added.

5. Finally, the method `paint()` is run. This method is used to output the results.

12.8   The do ... while loop

Example 88

```java
// Compute average of 5 numbers entered at the keyboard

import javax.swing.*;
import java.awt.*;

public class do1 extends JApplet
{
    Font f = new Font("SansSerif", Font.BOLD, 20);

    double n, total = 0.0, average;
    int c = 1;

    public void init()
    {
      do
      {
            String number = JOptionPane.showInputDialog
            ("Enter next number : ");
            n = Double.parseDouble(number);
            total += n;
            c++;
      }
      while (c <= 5);
      average = total / 5;
    }

    public void paint(Graphics g)
    {
      g.setFont(f);
      g.setColor(Color.DARK_GRAY);
      g.drawString("The average of 5 numbers entered = "
                  + average, 5, 40);
    }

}
```

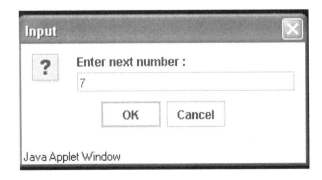

202

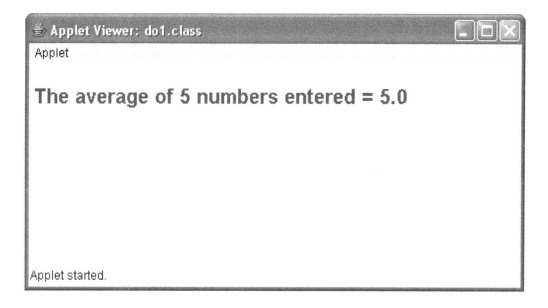

Notes:

1. A do while loop differs from a while loop in that the test to terminate the loop as at the end of the loop.

2. In this example, it may have been more sensible to use a for loop, as we are looping a fixed number of times.

3. When the calculation is complete, the results are output using a single `drawString()` statement from within the `paint()` method.

12.9 Using methods

<u>Example 89</u>

```java
import javax.swing.*;
import java.awt.*;

public class daysOfWeek extends JApplet
{
    Font f = new Font("SansSerif", Font.BOLD, 20);

    int n;
    String day;

    public void init()
    {
      String number = JOptionPane.showInputDialog
      ("Enter the day number : ");
      n = Integer.parseInt(number);

      day = getday(n);
    }


    public void paint(Graphics g)
    {
      g.setFont(f);
      g.setColor(Color.DARK_GRAY);

      g.drawString("Day " + n + " is " + day, 5, 40);
    }

    // Given a number 1 to 7, return the day of the week
    String getday(int n)
    {
      String day;
      switch (n)
      {
          case 1:       day = "Monday";      break;
          case 2:       day = "Tuesday";     break;
          case 3:       day = "Wednesday";   break;
          case 4:       day = "Thursday";    break;
          case 5:       day = "Friday";      break;
          case 6:       day = "Saturday";    break;
          case 7:       day = "Sunday";      break;
          default:      day = "Invalid day"; break;
      }
      return day;
    }

}
```

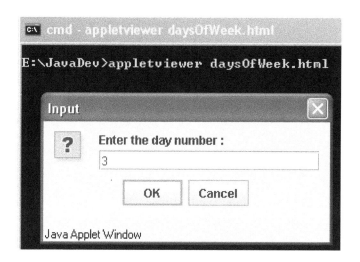

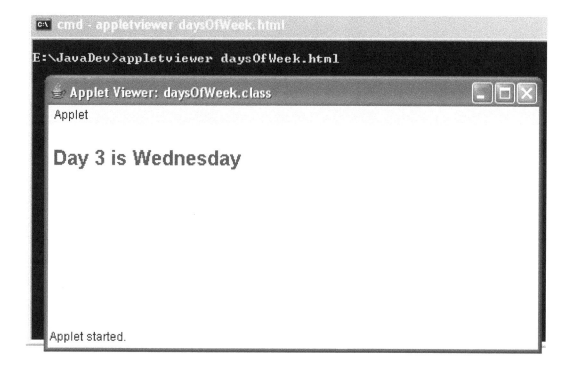

Notes:

1. A single user-defined method is used in this program. It has a single parameter – an int that is used to store the day-number. The return value is of type String. This is used to store the name of a day.

12.10   Using arrays

Example 90

```java
import javax.swing.*;
import java.awt.*;

public class Array extends JApplet
{
    Font f = new Font("SansSerif", Font.BOLD, 20);

    // An array of 10 doubles
    double a[] = {4, 5, 6, 7, 3, 6, 6, 7, 8, 9};
    double total = 0.0, min;
    int c;
    int x = 5;

    public void init()
    {
      // Sum elements of the array
      for(c = 0; c < 10; c++)
          total += a[c];

      // Display smallest element
      min = a[0];    // Start with first element as minimum
      for(c = 1; c < 10; c++)
          if(a[c] < min)
              min = a[c];
    }

    public void paint(Graphics g)
    {
      g.setFont(f);
      g.setColor(Color.DARK_GRAY);

          g.drawString("The numbers stored are: ", 5, 20);
          for(c = 0; c < 5; c++)
             g.drawString("" + a[c], (x+=50), 40);
          x = 5;
          for(c = 5; c < 10; c++)
             g.drawString("" + a[c], (x+=50), 60);

      g.drawString("The total of " + c + " numbers is "
                   + total, 5, 80);
      g.drawString("The minimum value is " + min, 5, 100);
    }
}
```

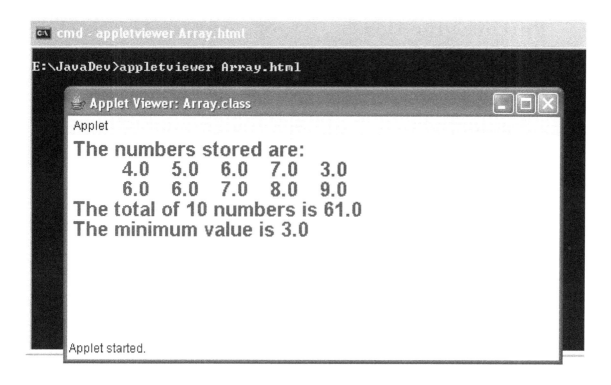

Notes:

1. The array a is of type double. So when you initialize it with a list of 10 integers, these will be converted to type double.

2. Within the init() method the 10 elements of the array are summed. Initially the variable total has a value of 0. Each element of the array is added to total giving the sum of the 10 numbers contained within the array.

3. The second section of code determines the minimum number. To start with the minimum value is assumed to be the first element. Then each element in the array is compared with the current minimum value (min). If the value is less than min, this value is assigned to min.

4. The paint() method is used to provide the output. As 10 values are to be displayed, I have decided to output 2 lines with 5 numbers in each. The output for each line uses a for loop.

5. Within the for loop, the counter c is used to select an element from the array. The problem we have, is that we need to specify the position for each number to be printed. In this case a variable x is used to determine the position in pixels. Each time x is incremented by 50. The expression x+= 50 has to be contained within brackets to force evaluation.

12.11   Further graphics

Drawing regular polygons requires us to do some mathematics to calculate the position of each of the corners.

If you were to construct a polygon manually you would perhaps draw a circle first. Any regular polygon can be fitted around a circle. It's just a matter of calculating the size of the angle turned at the centre of the circle. Then marking the corners around the edge of the circle by measuring equal angles from the centre.

To draw a hexagon on the screen we need to be able to compute the co-ordinates of each point. This is just a matter of using standard trigonometry.

1. You need to remember your trig ratios sine, cosine and tangent.

  (i) $\dfrac{x}{r} = \cos(60) \Rightarrow x = r \times \cos(60)$

  (ii) $\dfrac{y}{r} = \sin(60) \Rightarrow y = r \times \sin(60)$

2. Which you can evaluate using the sine and cosine functions.

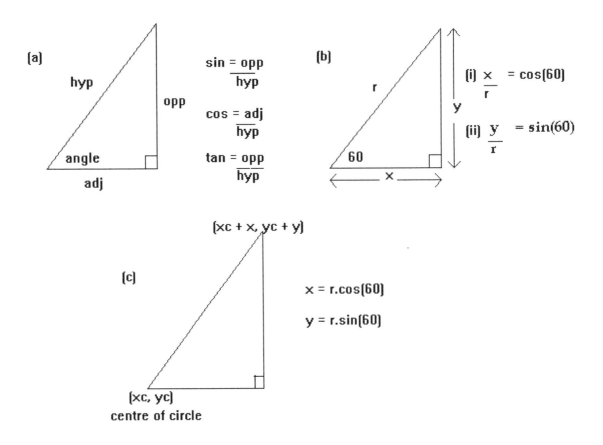

208

3. Having worked out distances x, and y we can now compute the new point by adding these values to the centre of the circle (xc, yc) to give:

nextpoint = (xc + r × cos(60), yc + r × sin(60))

4. We cannot directly code this directly in Java because the `Math.sin()` and `Math.cos()` methods take an angle expressed in radians, not degrees.

360 degrees = 2 × π radians

$\Rightarrow$ 1 degree = $\dfrac{2 \times \pi}{360}$ radians

$\Rightarrow$ 60 degrees = $\dfrac{2 \times \pi \times 60}{360}$ radians

5. To get successive points we have to turn through an angle of:

60, 120, 180, 240, 300, 360 degrees

A simple program to plot a hexagon may now look like this:

Example 91

```
import javax.swing.JApplet;
import java.awt.*;

public class Polygon2 extends JApplet
{
    public void paint(Graphics g)
    {
        int xc = 100, yc = 100, r = 80;
        int x[] = new int [6];
        int y[] = new int [6];

        for(int c = 0; c < 6; c++)
        {
            double angle = 2 * Math.PI * c * 60 / 360.0;
            x[c] = (int) (xc + r * Math.cos(angle));
            y[c] = (int) (yc + r * Math.sin(angle));
        }
        g.drawPolygon(x, y, 6);
    }
}
```

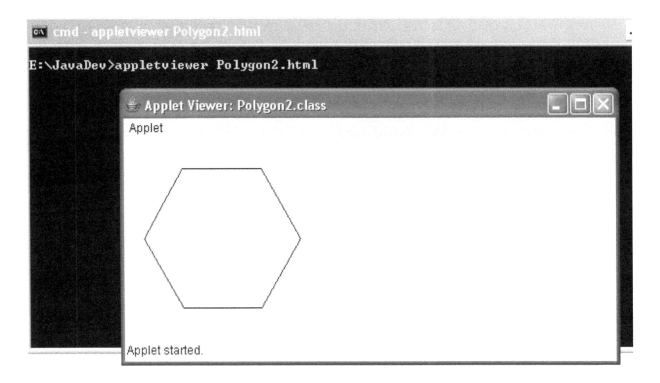

Notes:

1. A circle drawn with centre at the centre of any regular polygon will touch all of the corners. The angle at the centre between two neighbouring corners can be computed by dividing 360 by n, where n is the number of sides.

2. When using trigonometric functions within Java, and most other programming languages, the angles are always expressed in Radians. We will then have to convert our angles to radians using:

    2π radians = 360^0

3. We do not have to use an approximation for π, such as π = 3.142. A much more accurate value is contained within the Math class – Math.PI.

4. The angle turned each time = 360/6 = 60 degrees = 2π x 60 / 360 radians.

Exercise 12-1

1. The swing of a pendulum is a classic example of simple harmonic motion (SHM). The period of the motion denoted by T, is the time taken to return to the same spot in seconds. You can compute T with the following formula.

$$T = 2\pi \sqrt{\frac{l}{g}}$$ where l is the length in metres and, $g = 9.81 \text{ms}^{-2}$

Write a program that will allow a user to enter the length in m using an input dialog box. For the value of π, you can either use your own approximation, otherwise use `Math.PI`. Suitable output should be achieved using the `drawString()` method. Test your program with l = 2.5m and 0.75m.

2. A bank is to offer fixed-term (2 years) fixed rate savings bonds. The rate of interest depends on the amount being invested. The current rates are as follows.

Amount	£5000+	£10000+	£25000+
Rate	2.75%	3.15%	3.5%

Write a program that will allow a user to enter the amount they wish to invest. Use an input dialog box with a suitable prompt. From the amount entered, determine the rate of interest and calculate the amount that the bond will be worth in 2 years time assuming that interest is compounded annually. You can use the following formula.

$$FV = A(1 + \tfrac{R}{100})^n$$

Here FV is the future value of the investment, A is the amount invested, R is the rate of interest and n is the time in years.

You must use the `drawString()` method for all output, and this output should include the amount invested, the rate of interest and the future value after 2 years.

3. Write a program that will contain 3 methods `sinh()`, `cosh()` and `tanh()`. Each of these will have a single parameter – of type double and will return a double. The formulae for these methods are describe below.

```
sinh x = (eˣ - e⁻ˣ) / 2

cosh x = (eˣ + e⁻ˣ) / 2

tanh x = (eˣ - e⁻ˣ) / (eˣ + e⁻ˣ)
```

Test your methods, by entering a single value within an input dialog box. Output the results for x, `sinh(x)`, `cosh(x)`, and `tanh(x)` using the `drawString()` method.

Chapter 13 (Week 13)

Graphical user interfaces

13.1 GUI for applets

It is much easier to provide Graphical User Interfaces using applets, because the JApplet class inherits properties from the Panel class. A panel is like a window but also provides event-handling facilities.

Much of what is contained in this chapter can be found in chapter 8. In chapter 8 graphical user interfaces were created for Java applications. In this chapter graphical user interfaces are provided for Java applets. You will notice that there are many similarities and very few differences.

In particular, I have not taken the trouble to introduce the various components, layout managers or about the event-driven model, as this has already been described in chapter 8. Instead, I have illustrated how you will set up a graphical user interface using previously described components, but this time for applets.

13.2 Use of Buttons

In this example program two buttons will be created. A message will then be displayed indicating the last button clicked. Compare this with similar programs that were written using frames

Example 92

```
import javax.swing.*;
import java.awt.*;
import java.awt.event.ActionEvent;
import java.awt.event.ActionListener;

public class TestButton extends JApplet implements ActionListener
{
    JButton button1, button2;
    JLabel message;

    public void init()
    {
        setLayout(new FlowLayout());
        button1 = new JButton("button 1");
        add(button1);
        button1.addActionListener(this);
        button2 = new JButton("button 2");
        add(button2);
```

```java
        button2.addActionListener(this);
        message = new JLabel();
        add(message);

        setVisible(true);
    }

    public void actionPerformed(ActionEvent event)
    {
        if (event.getSource() == button1)
        {
            System.out.println("Button1 clicked!");
            message.setText("Current button is button1");
        }
        else if (event.getSource() == button2)
        {
            System.out.println("Button2 clicked!");
            message.setText("Current button is button2");
        }
    }

}
```

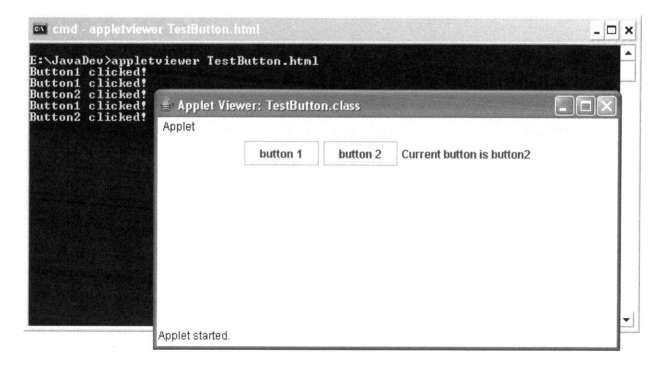

Notes:

1. The public class constituting the program inherits the properties of `JApplet` and also implements the `ActionListener` interface.

2. The applet, in which the program runs, acts as a container for placing components such as buttons and labels.

3. A class that implements the ActionListener interface acts like an event handler – it becomes responsive to events of this type.

4. The components are declared globally so that they can be accessed from any part of the program.

5. The initial set up – creation of components and registration of these components as an action listener takes place in the `init()` method which is the first method to execute.

6. There are two buttons and a label created. The label is used to store a message indicating which button has just been clicked.

7. The buttons are created using a `JButton()` constructor and added to the applet in much the same way as in chapter 8. The parameter for this constructor is the text that will appear on the button.

8. The label called message has not been given an initial value when it was created by the constructor `JLabel()`. This component is also is added to the applet.

9. The buttons need to be registered as an action listener as the user will interact with the buttons.

10. The `actionPerformed()` method is used to carry out the event-handling. It has a single parameter of type `actionEvent`.

11. Each time a button is clicked an event is generated of type actionEvent. The method `actionPerformed()` is called each time.

12. Within the method `actionPerformed()` it is necessary to determine which button was clicked. The value returned by the method `getSource()` identifies the name of the button clicked.

13. This is used in the if statement. There is a choice of two messages that can be used to update the text stored in the label called message. Which one is determined by the name of the button clicked. The method `setText()` is used to update the text of the label.

14. I have also included a `println()` statement in each part of the if statement. This displays a message on the console rather than within the applet. This technique is normally used for debugging purposes. In this case I have used it because I want to record which buttons I have clicked, not just the last button that I clicked.

13.3 Use of text fields and text areas

<u>Example 93</u>

```java
import javax.swing.*;
import java.awt.*;
import java.awt.event.ActionEvent;
import java.awt.event.ActionListener;
public class quadApp2 extends JApplet implements ActionListener
{
    JTextField aText, bText, cText;
    JLabel prompt, aLabel, bLabel, cLabel, answer;
    JButton button;
    int a, b, c;

    public void init()
    {
        setLayout(new FlowLayout());
        //Create labels and text boxes and add them to the applet
        prompt = new JLabel("Enter coefficients and press return");
        add(prompt);
        aLabel = new JLabel(" a ");
        add(aLabel);
        aText = new JtextField(3);
        add(aText);
        bLabel = new JLabel(" b ");
        add(bLabel);
        bText = new JtextField(3);
        add(bText);
        cLabel = new JLabel(" c ");
        add(cLabel);
        cText = new JtextField(3);
        add(cText);
        //Register text boxes as action listeners
        aText.addActionListener(this);
        bText.addActionListener(this);
        cText.addActionListener(this);

        //Add button
        button = new JButton(" OK ");
        add(button);
        button.addActionListener(this);

        //Add a label to store the answer
        answer = new Jlabel();
        add(answer);

        setVisible(true);
    }
```

```java
    public void actionPerformed(ActionEvent event)
    {
      if (event.getSource() == aText)
      {
          String aString = aText.getText();
          a = Integer.parseInt(aString);
      }

      if (event.getSource() == bText)
      {
          String bString = bText.getText();
          b = Integer.parseInt(bString);
      }

      if (event.getSource() == cText)
      {
          String cString = cText.getText();
          c = Integer.parseInt(cString);
      }

      if (event.getSource() == button)
      {
          double d = (double) (b * b - 4 * a * c);
          double d2 = Math.sqrt(d);
          double x1 = (-b + d) / (2 * a);
          double x2 = (-b - d) / (2 * a);

          answer.setText("x = " + x1 + " or x = " + x2);
      }
    }
}
```

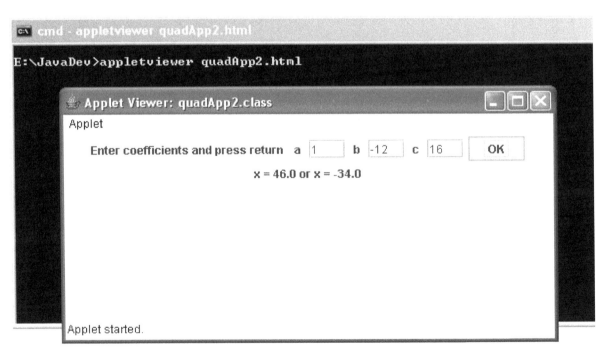

Notes:

1. As before, all components are declared globally so that they can be accessed by all methods.

2. All of the setup takes place in the `init()` method. This involves creating the components using an appropriate constructor, adding them to the applet, and in the case of the text boxes and the button, registering them as action listeners.

3. There are 3 text fields, one for each coefficient necessary for solving a quadratic equation. In front of each one a label is added so that the user knows what each of the text fields is for.

4. You indicate which text field you want to input with data by clicking on it with the mouse. You can then type in the value for that coefficient. You need to press return for the data to be accepted.

5. Pressing return when you have typed in the data generates an event which causes the method `actionPerformed()` to be run.

6. There are a number of if statements that test the value returned by the method `getSource()`. For each text box with data entered, a string is returned using the method `getText()`.

7. We need to extract the number entered within the string. The method `parseInt()` is used to achieve this.

8. Once all of the coefficients have been entered in the manner prescribed, the user needs to click on the button.

9. Clicking on the button creates an event which results in a calculation being performed. This calculation is based on the general formula for working out the roots of a quadratic equation. This is discussed in chapter 2 (2.9 Solving quadratic equations).

10. Once the calculation has been performed, the results are used to update the label called answer.

13.4   Check boxes and radio buttons

This example provides 3 checkboxes so that a user can indicate whether they have a degree, a teaching qualification and/or a driving licence. It also provides a group of radio-buttons so that they can indicate their marital status.

Example 94

```
import javax.swing.*;
import java.awt.*;
import java.awt.event.*;
import java.applet.*;

public class Pdetails extends JApplet
{
    JCheckBox degree, teachingQual, drivingLicense;

    JRadioButton single, married, divorced;
    ButtonGroup maritalStatus;

    public void init()
    {
        setLayout(new FlowLayout());

        //Create check boxes
        degree = new JCheckBox("degree");
        teachingQual = new JCheckBox("Teaching qualification");
        drivingLicense = new JCheckBox("Driving License");

        //Create radio buttons
        single = new JRadioButton("Single", false);
        married = new JRadioButton("Married", false);
        divorced = new JRadioButton("Divorced", false);

        //Add check boxes and radio buttons
        add(degree);
        add(teachingQual);
        add(drivingLicense);
        add(single);
        add(married);
        add(divorced);

        //Create Radio button group
        maritalStatus = new ButtonGroup();
        maritalStatus.add(single);
        maritalStatus.add(married);
        maritalStatus.add(divorced);

        //Create EventHandler object
        EventHandler eh = new EventHandler();
        //Register event handler with checkboxes and radio buttons
        degree.addItemListener(eh);
        teachingQual.addItemListener(eh);
```

```java
      drivingLicense.addItemListener(eh);
      single.addItemListener(eh);
      married.addItemListener(eh);
      divorced.addItemListener(eh);
   }

   private class EventHandler implements ItemListener
   {
      public void itemStateChanged(ItemEvent ie)
      {
          //Check each checkbox for a change of state
          if (ie.getSource() == degree)
              if (ie.getStateChange() == ItemEvent.SELECTED)
                  System.out.println("degree");

          if (ie.getSource() == teachingQual)
              if (ie.getStateChange() == ItemEvent.SELECTED)
                  System.out.println("Teaching qualification");

          if (ie.getSource() == drivingLicense)
              if (ie.getStateChange() == ItemEvent.SELECTED)
                  System.out.println("Driving license");
          repaint();
      }
   }

   public void paint(Graphics g)
   {
      int r = 50;
      if(degree.isSelected())
          g.drawString("Person has a degree",10, r+=20);

      if(teachingQual.isSelected())
          g.drawString("Person has a teaching qualification",10,
                     r+=20);

      if(drivingLicense.isSelected())
          g.drawString("Person has a driving license",10, r+=20);

      if(single.isSelected())
          g.drawString("Person is single", 10, r+=20);
      else if(married.isSelected())
          g.drawString("Person is married", 10, r+=20);
      else if(divorced.isSelected())
          g.drawString("Person is divorced", 10, r+=20);
   }
}
```

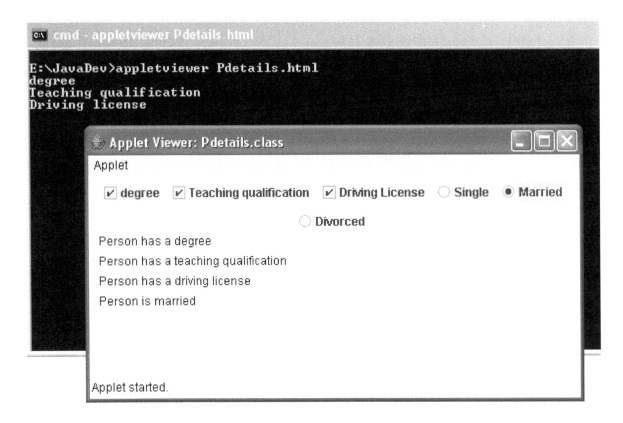

Notes:

1. The `init()` method is used to carry out all necessary actions before an event occurs. In particular it is used to create all check boxes and radio buttons.

2. A checkbox is used to indicate whether an individual has a degree, teaching qualification and/or driving license. This is because an individual can legitimately check any number of these items.

3. Single, married and divorced are mutually exclusive, so radio buttons are used.

4. A ButtonGroup object called maritalStatus links the 3 radio buttons.

5. All of the check boxes and radio buttons required to be registered as an ItemListener and are associated with an event handler called EventHandler.

6. Within the class EventHandler, the `itemStateChanged()` interface has been implemented. Here we can check the source of the event and whether the check box or radio button has been selected. In the example program, only the check boxes have been tested.

7. The method call `repaint()`, calls the `paint()` method.

8. Within the method `paint()` the status of each of the checkboxes is checked. If the check box or radio button has been selected, `drawString()` is used to print out this information.

13.5   Summary of GUI components

In this section I will summarize the swing components that we have already used in this chapter, and then mention other commonly used components that will appear later.

Label - A label is purely for displaying text. A swing label is created with the `JLabel()` constructor. You can give the label an initial text value when you create it, and you can update the value of the text within the label by using the method `SetText()`. A user cannot interact with a label directly.

Button - buttons are for clicking. A swing button is created with the `JButton()` constructor. When you create a button it is important to associate text with the button, otherwise a user will not know what they are clicking. As a user is expected to interact with buttons they have to be registered as an action listener, and the method `actionPerformed()` corresponding to this action listener interface must be implemented to test for events generated by buttons when they are clicked.

Text field - A text field is used to input text in a GUI environment. A swing text field is created with the `JTextField()` constructor. For a text field to be useful the `ActionListener` interface must be implemented. Each text field that is to respond to a user entering input, must be registered as an action listener. When a user enters text into a text field they must remember to press return. Pressing return fires an event that can be checked for within the method `actionPerformed()`.

Text area - is used to enter larger amounts of text that span several lines. A swing text area is created with the `JTextArea()` constructor. It is normal to have 2 parameters to specify the number of lines of text, and characters in each line. Like the text field, if a text area is to be useful it must be registered as an action listener. Also you will need to write code in the method `actionPerformed()` to check for this event together with appropriate actions should it be detected.

Checkbox - is a component which can be selected or deselected. A swing check box is created with the constructor `JCheckBox()`. It is normal to associate a label stating what the checkbox is for when you create it. If selected, the state of the control is marked as SELECTED and an event is fired that will run the event handler. If you click on the checkbox again, the checkbox will be deselected. This state can be checked for by the method `isSelected()` from within the event handling method `itemStateChanged()`.

CheckboxGroup - is a group of checkboxes. In a group of checkboxes only one of the checkboxes can be selected, as the checkboxes represent conditions which are mutually exclusive.

Radio buttons – A radio button looks a bit like a check box, except that they are round rather than square. Another important difference is that a group of radio buttons is mutually exclusive. That is, if one of the radio buttons has been selected, all of the others must be deselected. A swing radio button is created using the constructor `JRadioButton()`. The way you program radio buttons is also similar to that of a check box, as they are both item listeners.

Drop-down list – in swing this is referred to as a `JComboBox`. These are created using the `JComboBox()` constructor. The constructor used has a parameter of type `[] String`. The array contains a list of names that will appear in the pop-down menu. Only one item from the list can be selected.

13.6   drop-down lists

Example

```
import javax.swing.*;
import java.awt.*;
import java.awt.event.ActionEvent;
import java.awt.event.ActionListener;

public class Course extends JApplet implements ActionListener
{
    String [] courses = {"GCSE", "AS level", "A level",
                "BTEC first", "BTEC National", "Access to HE"};
    JComboBox courseList;
    JLabel message;

    public void init()
    {
        setLayout(new FlowLayout());

        courseList = new JComboBox(courses);
        courseList.setMaximumRowCount(3);
        add(courseList);
        courseList.addActionListener(this);

        message = new JLabel();
        add(message);

        setVisible(true);
    }

    public void actionPerformed(ActionEvent event)
    {
        if (courseList.getSelectedIndex() == 0)
            message.setText("Course chosen is GCSE");
        else if (courseList.getSelectedIndex() == 1)
            message.setText("Course chosen is AS level");
        else if (courseList.getSelectedIndex() == 2)
            message.setText("Course chosen is A2 level");
        else if (courseList.getSelectedIndex() == 3)
            message.setText("Course chosen is BTEC first");
        else if (courseList.getSelectedIndex() == 4)
```

```
            message.setText("Course chosen is BTEC National");
      else if (courseList.getSelectedIndex() == 5)
            message.setText("Course chosen is Access to HE");
  }
}
```

List once (1) has been clicked   (1) (2)

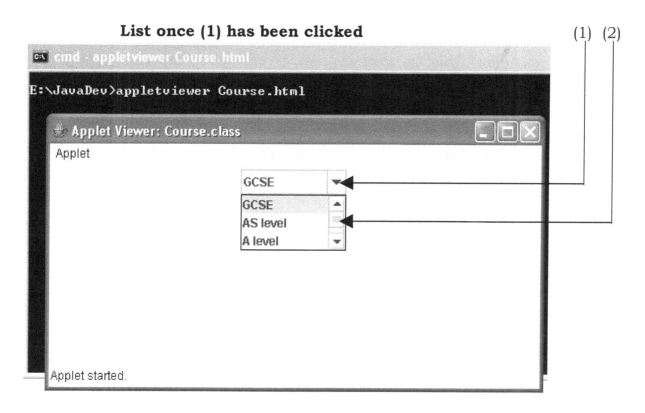

(1) Need to click here to get first 3 elements of the list
(2) Need to click on this scroll-bar to go up and down the list

List after last item has been selected

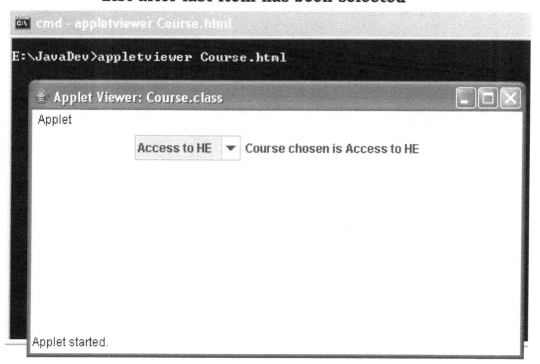

Notes:

1. The class Course implements the `ActionListener` interface. This is necessary because you want a user to be able to interact with the drop-down menu.

2. The list of courses available on the drop-down menu is implemented as an array of strings. This is passed as a parameter to the constructor `JComboList()`.

3. The `JComboList` class has a number of methods that affect the properties of a `JComboList` `object`. One of these is `setMaximumuRowCount()`. This method limits the number of items that are visible at any one time.

4. The `JComboList` object needs to be added to the applet and registered as an action listener.

5. A label is created for the purpose of storing a message that states which course has been chosen. This too has to be added to the applet, but does not have to be registered as an action listener as the user will not directly interact with the label.

6. When an item is clicked on the menu, an event is fired causing the method `actionPerformed()` to be run.

7. This method has a parameter which is an object of type ActionEvent.

8. Inside the method, the item selected is identified by using the method `getSelectedIndex()`. This returns the position of the selected item from the list of courses.

9. A return value of 0 indicates the first item from the list of courses, and so on. The if statement can then determine an appropriate message with which the label can be updated.

13.7 Using the mouse

Mouse events are generated when a user interacts with the GUI. They can be generated by any GUI component. For instance there are events that detect a change in position of the mouse, or whether the mouse button has been pressed or released. If the mouse button is pressed and then released, we say the mouse button has been clicked. There are events that can be used to detect all of these actions and more besides.

There are many classes that deal with windows events. For instance the `windowsEvent` class. This has 7 different types of event defined and for each of these there is a corresponding listener interface. The problem is, if we were to create a class based on this, we would have to write code for each event and the corresponding listener interface, regardless of whether we will want to make use of the events or not.

This justifies my use of the `MouseAdapter` class. With an adapter class, you don't have to implement all the events, just the ones you want to use. In the example program below, I am testing for two events – `mousePressed()` and `mouseReleased()`.

The program below makes use of pressing and releasing the mouse button, and also the current position of the mouse. In particular we are pressing the mouse button when we want to start drawing a line. The mouse is then moved to a new position and the button is released. A line is drawn between these two points.

Example 95

```java
import javax.swing.*;
import java.awt.*;
import java.awt.event.*;

public class TestMouse extends JApplet
{
    int mx, my;
    int mx1, my1;
    MouseHandler mh;
    boolean drawing = false;

    public TestMouse()
    {
      mh = new MouseHandler();
      addMouseListener(mh);

      setVisible(true);
    }

    private class MouseHandler extends MouseAdapter
    {
      public void mousePressed(MouseEvent e)
      {
          mx = e.getX();
```

```
                my = e.getY();
                drawing = true;
                repaint();
        }

        public void mouseReleased(MouseEvent e)
        {
                mx1 = e.getX();
                my1 = e.getY();
                drawing = true;
                repaint();
        }
    }

  public void paint(Graphics g)
  {
    g.drawString("(" + mx + "," + my + ")", mx, my);
    if(drawing==true)
    {
        g.drawLine(mx,my,mx1,my1);
        g.drawString("(" + mx1 + "," + my1 + ")", mx1, my1);
    }
    drawing = false;
  }
}
```

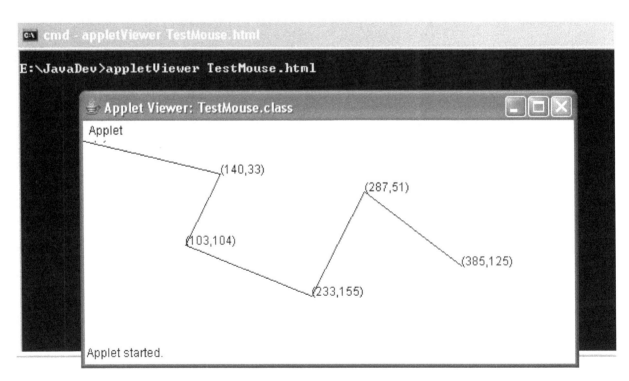

Notes:

1. Instance variables have been created to record the position of the mouse when the mouse button is pressed, and also when the mouse button is

226

released. When the mouse button is pressed the position of the mouse is given by (mx, mx), and when released the position is given by (mx1, my1).

2. When the mouse button is pressed, an event of type `MouseEvent` is generated, so that the method `mousePressed()` is run.

3. Within this method we are interested in locating the position. The method `getX()` is used to locate the x co-ordinate and the method `getY()` is used to locate the y co-ordinate.

4. When the mouse button is released, an event of type `MouseEvent` is generated. This time the method `mouseReleased()` is executed.

5. Within this method the x and y co-ordinates for the position of the mouse are determined in the same manner using `getX()` and `getY()`.

6. The method `paint()` is used for all output. In particular, if a mouse button is either pressed or released the co-ordinates are displayed on the screen using the `drawString()` method.

7. A line is drawn between the co-ordinates when the mouse was pressed and those co-ordinates when the mouse button was released. This is done using the `drawLine()` method.

8. There is a variable called drawing that is of type boolean. Its purpose is to determine when drawing should take place. In this case, between first pressing the mouse button and releasing it.

Exercise 13-1

1. Write an applet that will implement a counter in the following way. The applet should have a label and two buttons. The label is to be used to display the current counter value, starting with an initial value of 0. One of the buttons should be used to increment the counter by one the other should be used to decrement the counter by 1. These should be a check so that the counter can neither exceed 100, nor go lower than 0.

2. Write an applet which enables a user to:

   (a) enter the following information about themselves using text boxes

   > name, telephone number, date of birth

   (b) Indicate whether they live in rented property or own their own property using radio buttons.

   (c) Indicate whether they own any of the following possessions using check boxes

   > TV, video-player, mobile-phone, computer

   (d) includes a button to indicate that the information entered is correct

   (e) Implement the actionListener and itemListener interfaces, so that all of the components can interact with a user.

   (f) Implement the `actionPerformed()` method so that you can read the input entered into the text boxes and text area.

   (g) Implement the `itemStateChanged()` method. In it write an if statement that can be used to determine whether they rent or own property. In the same method determine the objects that the person owns.

   (h) Write a `paint()` method that can be called to output the data entered, displaying the data in an appropriate way using several `drawString()` statements.

Chapter 14 (week 14)   Example assignment

0.1   Assignment brief

Assignment for Unit 3

This assignment tests your ability to write Java applets. You will be expected to be able to perform basic arithmetic, use selection and iteration statements as well as arrays and methods. Finally you will be expected to write a program that uses a graphical user interface.

Task 1

To pass a course it is necessary to pass all three papers. For a given paper, to obtain a pass you must have achieved a mark of at least 40%. To pass the course overall you must have obtained an average mark of at least 50 %.

You are to use the following as test data:

Name	Maths	Science	Computer Science
Colmerauer, A	92	37	65
Hopper, G	71	56	45
Kemeny, J	51	46	43
Kernighan, D	56	59	83
Ritchie, D	60	78	89
Stroustrup, B	49	64	76
Wirth, N	87	74	82

a. Write a Java applet that will store the names, maths marks, science marks, and computer science marks in 4 separate arrays. You do not have to worry about keyboard input.

b. Create three more arrays. An array to store the minimum mark for each individual, an array to store the average mark for each individual, and an array to store "pass" or "fail".

c. Write a method called `getMin()` that will for any given individual, return the minimum mark for the 3 test papers sat. Store the minimum marks in the array intended for minimum marks.

d. Include in your program, code that can be used to compute the average score that an individual obtained for the 3 papers sat. Use this code to compute the average for each individual and store it in the array intended for average marks.

e. Use the minimum mark obtained together with the average score to determine whether an individual should pass or fail.

f. The output from this program should be obtained using several calls to the `drawString()` method. This should include name, maths mark, science mark, computer science mar, and whether they passed or failed.

Task 2

A bank is offering a rate of interest of 4.35% compounded monthly. You have £10000 to invest. You want to know in how many years will this sum be worth in excess of £20000.

You have seen in a book that compound interest can be calculated using the following formula.

$$FV = P(1 + R/100)^n$$

Here FV is the future value. This is what your investment will be worth in n years time. P is the principal. This is the amount of money you intend to invest. R is the rate of interest expressed as a percentage, and n is the number of years.

You realise that as the money is to be compounded monthly, you will need to adapt this formula.

$$FV = P(1 + R/1200)^{12n}$$

Here 12n represents the number of monthly payments. You may want to use the Math method `pow(x,y)`.

Write a program that will perform this calculation. You are required to output a whole number of years when the value of the investment exceeds £20000. As this is to be a general program, you are required to input values for the amount of money to be invested, and the rate of interest. Use input dialog boxes for the input.

Task 3

Modify your program for Task 2 so that a graphical user interface is provided for the user to interact. That is, in place of input dialogs use text fields, and for the output use labels. You will also need to include a button to indicate that all 3 values have been input before the calculation can proceed.

0.2   Task 1 solution

<u>Example 96</u>

```java
import javax.swing.*;
import java.awt.*;

public class Ass3_1 extends JApplet
{
    Font f = new Font("SansSerif", Font.BOLD, 20);

    int lineNum = 40;

    String [] name = {"Colmerauer, A", "Hopper, G",
                      "Kemeny, J", "Kernighan, D",
                      "Ritchie, D", "Stroustrup, D",
                      "Wirth, N"};

    int [] maths = {92, 73, 51, 56, 60, 49, 87};

    int [] science = {37, 56, 46, 59, 78, 64, 74};

    int [] compsci = {65, 45, 43, 83, 89, 76, 82};

    int minMark [] = new int [7];

    String grade [] = new String [7];

    double avMark [] = new double [7];

    public void init()
    {
      //Store minimum and average marks
      for(int c = 0; c < 7; c++)
      {
          int m = maths[c], s = science[c], cs = compsci[c];
          minMark[c] = getMin(m, s, cs);
          avMark[c] = (m + s + cs)/3.0;
      }

      //Determine whether a pass
      for(int c = 0; c < 7 ; c++)
      {
          if (minMark[c] >= 40 && avMark[c] >= 50)
              grade[c] = "pass";
          else
              grade[c] = "fail";
      }
    }

  public void paint(Graphics g)
  {
    g.setFont(f);
```

```
        g.setColor(Color.black);

        for( int c = 0; c < 7; c++)
        {
            g.drawString(name[c] + "   " + maths[c] + "    " +
                science[c] + "    "  + compsci[c] + "    " +
                grade[c], 5, lineNum);

            lineNum += 20;
        }
    }

    public int getMin(int m, int s, int cs)
    {
      int min = m;
      if (min > s)
          min = s;
      if (min > cs)
          min = cs;

      return min;
    }
}
```

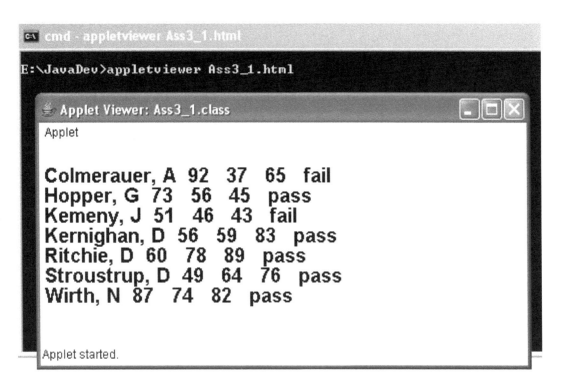

0.3　　Task 2 solution

<u>Example 97</u>

```java
import javax.swing.*;
import java.awt.*;

public class Ass3_2 extends JApplet
{
    Font font = new Font("SansSerif", Font.BOLD, 24);

    double finalAmount = 20000;
    double p, r;        //principal and rate
    int yr = 0;         //Number of years - initially 0
    double x;           //Ratio to multiply by p each month
    double y = 12;      //times interest is compounded per year
    double FV;

    int lineCount = 40;

    public void init()
    {

        String number1 = JOptionPane.showInputDialog
            ("Enter amount to invest in £ :");

        p = Double.parseDouble(number1);

        String number2 = JOptionPane.showInputDialog
            ("Enter rate of interest % :");

        r = Double.parseDouble(number2);

        x = (1 + r/1200);

        FV = p;

    }

    public void paint(Graphics g)
    {
      g.setFont(font);
      g.setColor(Color.DARK_GRAY);

      while (yr < 6)
      {
          FV = p * Math.pow(x, y);
          yr++;

          g.drawString("After year " + yr + " FV = " + FV, 5,
                        lineCount);
```

233

```
        lineCount += 20 ;
        p = FV;
    }
  }
}
```

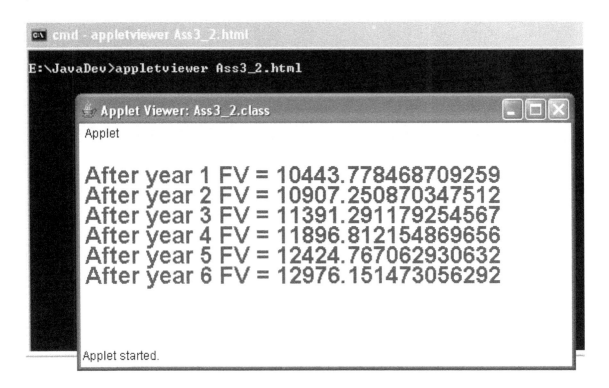

Notes:

The above program does not satisfy the specified task, though it may pass all of the assessment criteria that are asked for, as the same type of programming skills have been used.

You could think of this as a preliminary version that has been written to make sure that the formula is being applied correctly and that the interest is being added on each year. It is really a test version. The answers that have been output can then be verified by using a calculator.

Example 98

```java
import javax.swing.*;
import java.awt.*;

public class Ass3_2 extends JApplet
{
    Font font = new Font("SansSerif", Font.BOLD, 24);

    double finalAmount = 20000;
    double p, r;              //principal and rate
    int yr = 0;       //Number of years - initially 0
    double x;         //Ratio to multiply by p each month
    double y = 12;    //number of times interest is compounded per
                      //year
```

```java
    double FV;          //Future value

    int lineCount = 40;

    public void init()
    {
        String number1 = JOptionPane.showInputDialog
        ("Enter amount to invest in £ :");

        p = Double.parseDouble(number1);

      String number2 = JOptionPane.showInputDialog
      ("Enter rate of interest % :");

      r = Double.parseDouble(number2);

      x = (1 + r/1200);    //only needs to be evaluated once

      FV = p;                  //Intially FV = principal

      while (FV < finalAmount)
      {
         FV = p * Math.pow(x, y);
         yr++;
         p = FV;              //P for next year is current FV
      }
    }

    public void paint(Graphics g)
    {
      g.setFont(font);
      g.setColor(Color.DARK_GRAY);
      g.drawString("After year " + yr + " FV = " + FV, 5, 50);
    }
}
```

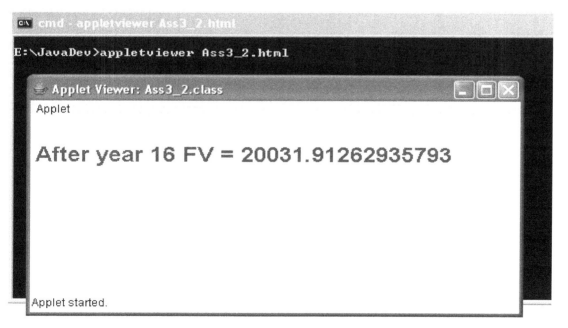

Task 3 solution

<u>Example 99</u>

```java
import javax.swing.*;
import java.awt.*;

public class Ass3_3 extends JApplet implements ActionListener
{
    Font font = new Font("SansSerif", Font.BOLD, 24);

    double fa;          //Amount that the future value must exceed
    double p, r;            //principal and rate
    int yr = 0;         //Number of years - initially 0
    double x;           //Ratio to multiply by p each month
    double y = 12;      //times interest is compounded per year
    double FV;

    //GUI components

    JLabel prompt;
    JLabel answer;
    JLabel pLabel, fvLabel, rLabel;
    JTextField initialAmount, finalAmount, interestRate;
    JButton button;

    public void init()
    {
        setLayout(new FlowLayout());

        //Create text boxes and  associated labels and
        //add them to the applet window

        pLabel = new JLabel(" P ");
        add(pLabel);
        initialAmount = new JTextField(10);
        add(initialAmount);

        fvLabel = new JLabel(" FV ");
        add(fvLabel);
        finalAmount = new JTextField(10);
        add(finalAmount);

        rLabel = new JLabel(" R % ");
        add(rLabel);
        interestRate = new JTextField(5);
        add(interestRate);

        //Register text boxes as action listeners

        initialAmount.addActionListener(this);
        finalAmount.addActionListener(this);
        interestRate.addActionListener(this);
```

```java
    //Add button and register this as an
    //action listener
    button = new JButton(" OK ");
    add(button);
    button.addActionListener(this);

    //Create answer label and add this to the applet window
    answer = new JLabel();
    add(answer);

    setVisible(true);
}

public void actionPerformed(ActionEvent event)
{
  if (event.getSource() == initialAmount)
  {
      String iAmount = initialAmount.getText();
      p = Double.parseDouble(iAmount);
  }

  if (event.getSource() == finalAmount)
  {
      String fAmount = finalAmount.getText();
      fa = Double.parseDouble(fAmount);
  }

  if (event.getSource() == interestRate)
  {
      String iRate = interestRate.getText();
      r = Double.parseDouble(iRate);
  }

  if (event.getSource() == button)
  {
      x = (1 + r/1200);    //only needs to be evaluated once

      FV = p;                 //Intially FV = principal

      while (FV < fa)
      {
          FV = p * Math.pow(x, y);
          yr++;
          p = FV;
      }

      answer.setText("In " + yr + " years time the future" +
                  " value will be " + FV);
  }
}
}
```

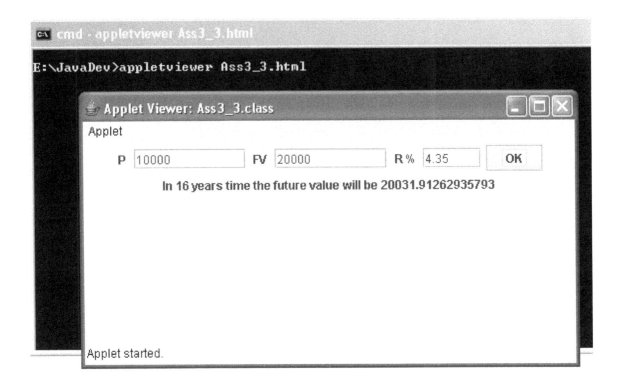

Notes:

1. The 3 text boxes are used for user input. When a user adds a value to one of these text boxes and presses return, an event is fired.

2. For the particular event detected, the string entered is converted to a double.

3. The data type double was chosen for each of the numbers. There is much less chance of the program crashing with this type. If an integer is entered it will be converted to a double.

4. When all 3 numbers have been entered, the user clicks on the OK button. This fires an event that carries out the calculation and displays the result in a label.

5. Ideally we would want to see the answer correct to 2 decimal places. If you use labels to display the output, you cannot make use of format specifiers that we made use of in conjunction with the printf statement. There are however other methods, but these are not covered in this book.

Chapter 15 (week 15)

15.1   Tasks to finish

This week is reserved for finishing off your assignment. All of these programs for this assignment will be Java applets rather than Java applications. For each Java applet you are required to write you will need an HTML file that has an appropriate `<applet>` tag, so that you can run the applet.

It is recommended that you write a template HTML file to run applets. Then all you need to do is change the name of the class file that is to be run.

You will need to write at least one applet that does not implement a graphical user interface (GUI). In this case, you will be expected to use input dialog boxes for keyboard input and the `drawString()` method from within `paint()` for all output generated.

For this type of applet you will be tested on a number of programming techniques that can also be found in parts 1 and 2 of the book. These could include performing arithmetic calculations, using selection statements, repetition, arrays and methods.

For at least one of the applets you will be expected to implement a simple graphical user interface using swing components. As it is likely that you will be including more than one component, you will have to use a layout manager.

To be useful to a user, you will need to implement a listener interface and register all active components with this interface so that a user can interact with these components

15.2   End of unit summary

1. Applets are Java programs that are called from within a web page (HTML file).

2. The program appletviewer allows you to run an applet without having to load a web page. Typically appletviewer is used to test Java applets.

3. An applet is called from an HTML file using the `<APPLET>` tag.

4. Nowadays applets are created using the JApplet class. This is part of the swing Package.

5. Each Java applet must have the statement import `javax.swing.JApplet;` or import `javax.swing.*;` to create an applet.

6. Each applet automatically has the methods `init()`, `start()`, `stop()` and `destroy()`. These are called at various stages of the applet life-cycle.

7. The `paint()` method is used to carry out all output to the applet.

8. The `paint()` method has a single parameter of type `Graphics`. This object of type Graphics is used to call methods such as `drawString()` and `drawLine()` etc.

9. The `drawString()` method is used to display strings on an applet.

10. It is very easy to draw simple images using a number of methods within `paint()`. You can for instance draw lines, rectangles, ovals and polygons. For each of the methods used to draw a closed shape, there are corresponding methods to draw a filled shape.

11. When writing programs that do calculations, selection, iteration, arrays or methods, the way you do so is exactly the same as for Java applications. In this part of the book, these topics are covered, but not in much detail. You can always refer to parts 1 and 2 of the book for other examples and explanations of these topics.

12. In this chapter, these topics are covered merely for completeness, and also to demonstrate how you will use the `paint()` method for output in a number of different situations.

13. Later on in this part of the book we also looked at graphical user interfaces. Many of the ideas we used in part 2 of the book also apply to applets. Exactly the same GUI components that were used for Java applications can be used for Java applets.

14. Like Java applications, for a user to be able to interact with GUI components within an applet, a listener interface must be implemented, and all active components must be registered with this.

15. The main difference is that we do not need to create a container such as a JFrame object to contain the GUI components, as a JApplet object is a type of window and behaves like a container.

Bibliography

Java programming books

Anderson, Julie & Franceschi, Herve. Java 5 illuminated. Jones and Bartlett 2005

Cohoon, James & Davidson, Jack. Java 1.5 Program Design. McGraw-Hill 2004

Deitel, H.M & Deitel P.J. Java How to program 5/e. Prentice-Hall 2003

Farrell, Joyce. Java programming 3/e. Thomson Course Technology 2006

Horton, Ivor. Ivor Horton's Beginning Java 2: JDK 5 Edition. Wrox 2005

Hubbard, John R. Programming with Java 2/e. McGraw-Hill 2004

Lewis, John & Loftus, William. Java software solutions: Foundations of program design 4/e. Addison-Wesley 2005

Malik, D.S. Java programming: From problem analysis to program design 2/e. Thomson Course Technology 2006.

Sierra, Kathy & Bates, Bert. Head first Java 2/e. O'Reilly 2005

Skansholm, Jan. Java from the beginning 2/e. Addison-Wesley 2004

Computer Science books

Teukolsky, Roselyn. AP Computer Science: levels A and B 4/e. Barron's educational services inc 2008.

Mathematics books

Banks, Tony & Alcorn, David. Mathematics for Edexcel GCSE Higher Tier 1/e. Causeway press 2001

Croft, Anthony & Davison, Robert & Hargreaves, Martin. Introduction to Engineering Mathematics 1/e. Addison-Wesley 1995

Index

unary operators 25
unicode 16
uppercase 32

V

validation 56-57
`valueOf()` 33
variable
      assignment 18-19
      declaration 17
      naming 17
variance 99
verification 56, 57-58
void keyword 14

W

while loop 65
whitespace
windowsEvent class 225
wrapper classes 34-35

www.ingramcontent.com/pod-product-compliance
Lightning Source LLC
Chambersburg PA
CBHW081225050326
40689CB00016B/3687